PUBLIC RELATIONS
FOR YOUR BUSINESS

For a complete list of Management Books 2000 titles,
visit our web-site on http://www.mb2000.com

PUBLIC RELATIONS FOR YOUR BUSINESS

Frank Jefkins

This edition revised and updated by James Alexander

Ill.
2000

First published in 1987 by Mercury Books

This revised edition published 2000 by Management Books 2000 Ltd
Cowcombe House
Cowcombe Hill
Chalford
Gloucestershire GL6 8HP
Tel. 01285 760 722
Fax. 01285 760 708
E-mail: mb2000@compuserve.com

Printed and bound in Great Britain by Biddles, Guildford

British Library Cataloguing in Publication Data is available
ISBN 1-85252-347-6

Foreword

by Warren Newman, FIPR
President of the Institute of Public Relations, 1987

Frank Jefkins was the friend of public relations students for many years. His clarity of expression, knowledge of the profession and its techniques, and combination of theory with good practical examples have endeared him to generations of young practitioners who gained their first insights by means of his books. In Public Relations for Your Business he brought that same deft touch to explaining to potential users of public relations something of what they can expect for their money and how to get the best out of professional advisers.

A crucial point to understand when reading this book is that you do not have any option other than to communicate. All individuals and all businesses have relationships with a host of other individuals and organisations. The outcome of those relationships is a reputation – or public relations. You are bound to have a reputation. The only choice you have to make is whether it emerges by accident or as a result of a deliberate process.

Professional public relations advisers believe that a planned effort to develop a reputation is likely to yield better results than one which happens without any thought. This book will show you how many different kinds of audiences you need to be concerned about and how, first identifying them, and then planning your communications with them, can pay great business dividends.

A simple illustration is how an organisation looks (Chapter 3). All organisations have to order things like stationery, signs, crockery, brochures and so on. If every manager has to decide every time what colour such things should be, what typeface should be used, and how things should be laid out, the result is both time-consuming and does not give a corporate feel to the organisation. Contrast that with a visit to McDonalds, where every item you see and touch is graphically co-ordinated. It gives a unified impression of a firm which can manage itself efficiently – exactly what they want to convey. Apart from the initial design costs, applying a visual identity which delivers a positive impression is no more expensive than a random, unplanned approach.

The same is true in all the facets of public relations. No organisation would dream of not managing its finances or its staff: why should managing your reputation be any less important?

Before you can get the best out of your public relations advisers – whether they be on your staff or consultants – you must be able to define clearly the task you want them to carry out. This book will help you to do that. PR comes in all shapes and sizes and with a price-tag to match. You will have to judge the level of advice you need according to the problem you wish to solve or the aspect of your communications you wish to manage. The person you approach to help you promote a product is probably quite different from the one you should be talking to about managing your lobbying of parliament or setting up a community relations programme.

By the end of this book I hope you will cringe just a little when you hear people saying 'Oh, it's just a public relations exercise'. You will know that a PR programme involves deserving a good reputation and then putting a lot of effort into trying to enjoy a reputation that you deserve.

Preface to the new edition

This is not an academic textbook. It is aimed at those in business, whatever type of business, who want to know how public relations applies to them and their business. People are often surprised to find that PR is not quite what they thought it was. Here they can discover the many ways in which PR can enhance business success; or the book may confirm that they are good communicators and doing all the right things.

This book seeks to take the mystery out of PR, and present it as a practical aspect of good business. It demolishes a great many myths about PR and gives many examples of its successful application. Some of the content may be controversial. Readers may not always agree with what is said. But it will make them think why and how PR is their business.

A number of things have changed since the author wrote the first edition of this book, not least in the tremendous advances in information technology and the rapid proliferation of computers, insinuating themselves into every facet of business life. This book has been thoroughly revised with that in mind, but the underlying principles remain solid and immensely practicable.

New people have come into PR and with them has come a wealth of new ideas and creativity. The manager of any business, whether it is just old Fred Fernackerpans and his window-cleaning business or the boss of a multi-national, multi-faceted conglomerate, ignores good public relations at his peril.

Those computer-literate entrepreneurs who have started dotcom businesses and have paved the way for a global explosion in e-commerce are just as much in need of good PR as more traditional businesses. Likewise, traditional business, whether small or vast, who have embraced the delights of the internet, will find that they have a new medium through which to develop sound PR practices.

The basic principles are the same for all. Read on ...

Please note that we have used 'he' or 'she' ad lib in this book rather than repeatedly using the awkward 'he or she' everywhere. In any case, the opposite gender is equally applicable.

CONTENTS

1

Do I Need PR?

'You ask me what it is l do. Well actually, you know,
I'm partly a liaison man and partly PRO.
Essentially I integrate the current export drive
And basically I'm viable from ten o'clock till five.'

Sir John Betjeman, Executive

First, what do you mean by PR? Whether or not you need PR depends on either what PR means to you or what it actually means. They could be two different things. They probably are.

Let us be clear about what the initials represent. They could stand for either press relations or public relations, and there are rather illiterate journalists who talk about 'a PR' when they mean a PRO. The first (press relations) is a part of the second (public relations), and the third (a PR) is bad English.

Public relations means different things to different people, but professionally it means:

the deliberate, planned and sustained effort to establish
*and maintain **mutual understanding***
between an organisation and its public.

Very simple, really, except that understanding is probably the most difficult thing in the world to achieve. It is a process of effecting change. To clear away the debris of misunderstanding and myths about PR, let's begin by demolishing three of them.

> **Myth no 1 – Public relations is a form of advertising – free advertising.**

Oh, no it's not!

Did you think or wish it was? It is not uncommon for business people, who understand and use advertising, to think of PR as a way of getting something for nothing. But the two are very different, and in any case, you get nothing for nothing in this world. At least PR costs time, and time costs money.

PR is very time consuming because it is labour intensive and you have to work very hard at it to achieve results.

Press relations will be dealt with in Chapter 4 but it is worth stating at the beginning of this book that the majority of news releases are rejected by editors because they are advertisements. The trouble is that a lot of business people insist that news releases be written like advertisements, but that is the kiss of death. We shall return to this in Chapter 4, but you might want to read that chapter now if you think press relations is about free advertising.

Advertising and PR

The main distinction between advertising and PR is that:

- **advertising aims to persuade in order to sell**, but
- **PR aims to inform in order to educate.**

They are two different forms of communication, legitimate in their own ways, but with different purposes and often aimed at different people.

> **Myth no 2 – Public relations is a means of white-washing, or pretending that things are better than they are.**

<u>Oh, no it's not</u>!

It is a naive misuse of PR to expect it to provide a smoke-screen when things go wrong, thinking that PR tactics can be applied in a trouble-shooting role. This is exactly what the media expect of PR, so little do they understand it, as can be seen when they express their scepticism of a political initiative by dismissing it as a 'PR exercise'.

Myth no 3 – PR is intangible, its results incapable of assessment.

<u>Oh, no it's not</u>!

Fortunately this myth has largely lost credence, probably because hard-headed business people in periods of recession expect value for money. They have even found PR better value for money than advertising, as we have seen with some of the major sponsorships such as Canon's three-year sponsorship of the Football League. It culminated in the proud boast that almost every British office had a Canon machine. It is a shame that Canon's excursions into advertising in China in 2000 were not so carefully thought out politically.

The secret, as in every aspect of business, lies in planning. A planned PR programme has to have objectives, and either those results are achieved or they are not. You plan to arrive at your office, and either you do or you don't. Cost-effective PR works the same way.

We shall return to this in Chapter 9 when we consider whether it is worth having an in-house PR department.

If PR is *not* a substitute for expensive advertising, if it is *not* a means of waving a magic wand when things go wrong, and if it is *not* intangible, what is it and why is it needed by business people? Perhaps too much mystery has been created about PR, too much glamour has been attached to PR consultancies, and too many PROs have been depicted as charlatans in books and films. Who was it cried out in despair, 'If I meet another man who says he's in PR, I'll simply scream!'?

The fact is that PR exists in any organisation whether we like it or not, for it is no more than the communications of human relations. It is like the weather and it won't go away. But what business people need is good PR, that is, effective communications which produce good human relations.

This truism applies to any type of business. As you read through the book, you will find a wealth of ideas and examples of how PR works. But you might say, 'that cannot possible apply to me!' This may be because you are quite a small organisation and could not afford huge amounts of money to set up such schemes, or you may feel that this or that idea is not applicable to your type of enterprise. No problem – take each idea and look at it from a different point of scale. If we say that an *international* advertising programme might be sensible, read 'within my town or community'. If the talk is of hiring in a PR consultancy, then think of it as asking a colleague or a neighbour with a flair for publicity what he or she thinks. All the pointers in the book have validity, even if the scale may be rather daunting for a small business. Better to try something modest than to miss the opportunity of spreading your message and not increasing your business.

One source defines PR people as 'reputation managers'. This is a neat condensation of the concept. Let us look at it in detail.

With whom?

Advertising is aimed at limited targets such as distributors and consumers. It is primarily to do with selling. It is a part of the marketing mix. But PR ranges more widely since a business is not only concerned with selling. This is where confusion sets in: surely the primary object of a business is to sell its goods and services and make a profit? That is true, but none of that can happen economically and efficiently unless every other facet of the business plays its part. A chain is as strong as its weakest link: PR can ensure that every link in the chain is strong.

The links in the business chain consist of its employees, production units, suppliers of services and materials, shareholders, distributors and customers, and in some organisations there may be other links. The whole chain must operate perfectly at full stretch. If

PR is limited to the marketing link, as often happens, what happens to the other links? This is where the PR-minded chief executive can be such an asset to the organisation because he can see PR as being involved throughout the organisation. In such companies, the PRO is answerable to him, not to one of the link managers such as the marketing manager. This kind of CEO has recognised the need for PR in the fullest sense. It happens in our most successful companies where PR functions at board level.

This leads back to the question, do you – as a business person – need PR? This question is not confined to whether you need a PRO, a PR department, or a PR consultant. You should be a PR person yourself, and it should be part of your job specification as someone working in business. The PR philosophy of creating understanding should be part of your managerial philosophy, even though you may need skilled technicians or practitioners to undertake the specialised PR work. Ask yourself – does your reputation need managing?

To be successful, you need to be a good communicator and to know how to buy and use the talents and services of communication specialists. The captain has to be a good sailor, but he also needs a crew of specialist sailors.

Public relations is thus a quality of leadership

Is this surprising? Some business leaders take the attitude of 'Why keep a dog and bark yourself?' They relegate the PRO to a position of lowly authority and status. Yet in many of our major companies those being groomed for top management have to head up the PR department for three years on their way to the top. This is a realistic approach to PR.

The reason for this is clear when you accept public relations for what it basically is – creating mutual understanding between the organisation and the world at large. Most industrial disputes, poor product design, bad distribution, poor customer relations, bad political relations, depressed share prices and even take-over bids result from lack of mutual understanding. The same applies to many of the problems of the world in which we live. A lot of this misunderstanding is at board level.

15

PR versus negative situations

This can be explained if we look at the four negative situations or states with which PR has to deal, the heart of the PR task. They are *hostility, prejudice, apathy* and *ignorance.* Most PR programmes are about converting these negative states into positive ones, resulting in the ultimate purpose of PR, understanding. That leads to goodwill and reputation. Understanding is often to do with perception of behaviour. How well is your company seen to behave – how well is its behaviour understood?

The answer to the question, 'do I need PR?', lies in the extent to which your organisation suffers from some or all of those four negative states of hostility, prejudice, apathy and ignorance.

Or don't you believe they exist? Are you positive that everyone who matters to your business – and have you ever considered who they are? – loves you, is unprejudiced, is interested in you, and is well-informed about who you are and what you do? You should be so lucky! Like poor Narcissus, you could be hooked on a mirror image which is a fallacy.

So there's a smack in the face for you. Before planning a PR programme it is necessary to discover the current image, that is what outsiders and your own staff think about your organisation. They might not be thinking anything at all!

✗ Hostility ✗

Most organisations suffer from some degree of hostility. There is, for instance, the 'Big is Bad' syndrome. Bigness usually results from a blend of astute management and popularity of products or services. Coca-Cola, IBM, Ford, Nestle, ICI and other giants would not be as big as they are if they did not have a well-organised system of production and distribution and people did not like their products. They have also looked after their public relations. Nevertheless, big corporations do attract hostility, simply because they are big and successful, especially if they are multi-nationals. Sometimes they can be too big and unsuccessful and lose a major contract.

But hostility can occur for other quite irrational reasons, usually based on misunderstanding, and the fondly held internal mirror image will not reveal them. There may be hostility towards a company because of its national parentage – British, American, Japanese, for instance. Or because of the company or brand name, packaging, price, method of distribution or after-sales services, all forms of marketing communications. Or hostility because of the company's alleged materials sourcing or manufacturing policies – ask McDonalds about that!

Bad industrial relations can produce hostility among customers. Adverse media stories can do likewise as can political or social allegiances that the public view with some dislike.

Many companies are vulnerable to criticism and attack. There may be environmental and pollution problems, and the company may be the victim of articulate protest. Swiss and German pharmaceutical companies have had this problem. In Britain, British Nuclear Fuels has been the victim, rightly or wrongly, of hostility born of public fear. Believing in itself, BNFL has mounted vigorous PR campaigns, more than ever needed in 1999/2000 because of poorly checked and mis-labelled nuclear material destined for Japan. The company was faced with a huge battle to restore its credibility, particularly as their main product line is so disliked and distrusted by so many people. It took a £40m compensation settlement to restore BNFL's status as a creditable player in nuclear re-processing.

Hostility can therefore be a very real threat to goodwill, reputation and successful operation at all levels from staff recruitment to share price, let alone sales.

Prejudice

Prejudice is the result of upbringing and environment so that it can be difficult to combat, and yet a business may not be able to succeed and survive unless prejudice against it and its products or services is overcome. The Japanese have been very clever at this, especially in the Asiatic countries which they occupied during the Second World War. Japanese cars are no longer burnt in the streets of Jakarta, and Malaysia has its 'Look East' policy, and has built the Proton car with support from Mitsubishi. You don't see many British motor-cars in Hong Kong, Jakarta, Kuala Lumpur or Singapore. The prejudice has turned the other way, as exemplified by the 1990s policy in Malaysia of 'Buy British Last'.

Do you need PR to overcome prejudice?

Some companies find it difficult to recruit staff because of prejudice about their industry or trade. The chemical industry and science as a whole has had this problem with young people. In Holland, Philips built their marvellous Evoluon exhibition centre to inspire youthful interest in science. Lloyds Bank had a videotape starring James Bellamy to overcome the prejudice of school-leavers that banks are dull places in which to work. Rentokil had to fight the prejudice that woodworm existed only in homes which were dirty. Years ago, grapefruit importers had to break the prejudice that the fruit was sour tasting.

In the late 1980s, Eddie Shah was confronted by the prejudice that colour pictures belonged to magazines rather than to newspapers. The same attitude occurred when colour television arrived, and people were for a long time happy to continue to accept black and white. Packaged holiday tour promoters had to fight prejudices against foreign foods, languages and currencies. There are people who will not fly. There is still a considerable prejudice against buying goods on the internet, but that will change as the security and convenience aspects are ironed out. An astonishingly large percentage of UK residents still say that they have no intention whatever of becoming involved in the internet, for buying things least of all.

That emphasises a common psychological factor – that people prefer the things they know best. People tend to be conservative, to play safe. In this, PR can be valuable in familiarising people with the unfamiliar.

Had you thought about PR in this way? A bit different from bang-the-drum, blow-the-trumpet advertising.

⚡ Apathy ⚡

Are people apathetic about your products or services? Is there a market for you if only you could break this apathy? Great businesses have been built on beating the apathy bug. Insurance companies are doing it today with direct response marketing. The British Telecom flotation was the first to tackle the smaller shareholder. Rentokil's fame and fortune was partly built on tackling the apathy about protecting the timber in one's home. Cable television was perhaps one of the biggest contenders in the apathy stakes.

Public relations can do more to counteract apathy than advertising because it is more subtle and credible. Apathy, or lack of interest, is defensive, the wagon-circle effect. It is like the snail retreating into its shell. Advertising is too clumsy and brash to entice the snail to re-emerge. Public relations, because it is not persuasive or biased, can provoke curiosity and interest and undermine apathy. Maybe, after that has been achieved, advertising can play its persuasive role and induce action.

But PR precedes the action. No one is going to take action – that is, buy – unless their interest has been whetted and their confidence has been created. Advertising may be able to do these things – but at what a cost! Advertising has today become one of the most expensive forms of communication, and this can mean that it is not cost-effective. The cost difference can often be resolved by the use of PR which is not only less expensive but more cost-effective because it works.

This is not to say that public relations is a soft sell. It isn't any kind of sell. That's the business of advertising.

Has all that puzzled you? Did you think public relations was to do with persuasion, was biased and a soft sell? There are people, even in PR, who think this way but they are short-changing themselves. These are counterfeit notions of PR.

Advertising is in the persuasion business – it is entitled to be biased, and it can use quicker hard-sell techniques, but we are not talking about advertising. That's another world. Forget it if you want to know whether you need PR.

Public relations and advertising are like the telephone and the megaphone, related yet different forms of communication, a two-way and a one-way system.

⚡ Ignorance ⚡

This leads on to the problem of ignorance, every business person's enemy in more than one way.

Ignorance is the product of an increasingly complex world. No-one is a walking encyclopaedia. You know your business inside out. You eat and sleep it. Outsiders are not only apathetic but must, inevitably, know far less about it than you do. Advertising may tell them something about it, but people have to take the trouble to read your advertisements.

With public relations, the effort can be negligible. People can enjoy reading about your subject in a feature article or watching a video, being aware of your sponsorship, seeing your tape on television, hearing about you on the radio. In other words, they can learn about your organisation, product or service in a leisurely, more participatory fashion. It is an educational, and sometimes an entertaining process. This may be through what is known as market education. See more about this in chapter 13.

People now know much more about computers because there are television programmes, newspaper and magazine articles, endless e-commerce mentions on radio and television and more and more general conversation about computers, web sites and the like. Children are now often more competent than their parents and PCs have become part of most people's lives. There are also numerous magazines devoted to computers, both domestic and industrial. The PC is now on countless office desks, and the old typewriter is now as rare as hen's teeth. Public relations has played a big part in this transformation, familiarising people with the unfamiliar and often forbidding.

So, how ignorant are people about your business? Perhaps you should find out. Cornhill Insurance conducted a survey which showed that 80% of the adult male population had never heard of them. That was why they sponsored test cricket some years ago. It worked handsomely for them.

You may not be in that sort of league. Perhaps you are a sprat or a mackerel and not a whale of an insurance company. A local shopkeeper may realise that, though he has an excellent shop, there are potential customers who are ignorant of his existence. A simple PR effort like a local newspaper story about his enterprising way of selecting stock, or why he went into business, or how his family contributes to the business, could attract interest far superior to any advertisement. Similarly, a larger business can overcome ignorance about its activities if they can be discovered through editorial features or other PR methods. It is simply a matter of scale.

PR versus sales resistance

Here is a story to prove the point. A certain company wanted to sell its products and services to local authorities. There was sales resistance in the forms of all four of our negative states of hostility, prejudice, apathy and ignorance. Even the company's sales manager was sceptical. Local authorities were happy to go their own way, and did not want to deal with a commercial company. The managing director of the company saw both the PR prestige value of being seen to supply local authorities and the huge volume of sales it could bring him. Here was the sort of conflict and challenge which PR relishes.

A PR programme was conducted using videos, technical conferences and press relations. The conferences were held in strategic towns and cities throughout the UK. Relevant local government officers were invited to attend. The conferences took the form of a one-day school with four technical speakers and four documentaries. There were no advertising or product displays, although the identity of the organisers and the purpose of the conference was explained in the invitation. Lunch and refreshments were provided. The talks and documentaries dealt objectively with technical problems and their solutions, and the programme was informative, interesting and helpful to the guests. The solutions were often based on research and product developments. They were so in advance of the methods practised by local authorities that the company was able to convey its message that it was advantageous for its services and products to be adopted by the guests. It was a very convincing operation, and something which could not have been done through advertising, which would have been premature anyway.

The press relations campaign was conducted through a municipal magazine. The company was servicing a few local authorities. They gave permission for articles to be written, illustrated by photographs showing the company's staff carrying out the service, and a series of articles was published.

The results of this educational campaign were impressive. Within two years, service contracts and product sales were operating with a large number of local authorities. This was extended to other public services such as hospitals, and today it is a very well-established side of the company's business. In fact, much of this business was derived from recommendations, in itself a valuable form of public relations. This new business development also contributed to the company's excellent share price performance, and the company is today the undisputed leader in its field. It has gained some major contracts and the company has expanded internationally.

The real point of this story is that both the source of new business and the use of PR were the inspiration of the managing director. He had no doubt that he needed PR if he was to win that new business and the spin-off PR effect it would have on the company's corporate image.

2

Do I Need a Corporate Image?

'There is nothing makes a man suspect much, more than to know little.'

Francis Bacon

A favourable image

No doubt you would like a favourable image for your business. Who doesn't? The question is, does the business warrant one?

What is your trading record?

- If you made a loss last year, you are not likely to convince anyone, from your secretary to an investment analyst in the City, that you are financially stable – let alone an investment prospect.

- If you had an unhappy industrial dispute, it may be difficult to keep or recruit staff, or win contracts which depend on prompt delivery.

- If a product proved faulty and had to be recalled, you will have problems with prospective customers. Some of the early online banks can testify to that.

- Maybe your advertising offended against the British Code of Advertising Practice, and the Advertising Standards Authority ruled against you. That was nasty publicity.

23

- You may be in some kind of service industry where it is difficult to please everyone all the time; critics may abound, as happens with the energy industries, the Post Office, transportation companies and even British Telecom.

- Perhaps you want to go public, but the City and the punters know little about you. Not so easy, is it, to achieve a favourable image?

What is a corporate image?

The point about a good image is that it has to be earned. You cannot go out and buy it like a new suit. Some people think you can 'make' an image. You cannot.

Think about it for a moment. What is your image of Tuvalu, The Acadamie Française, the Performing Rights Society or even the Institute of Public Relations? The chances are you have none, or the wrong one, or something pretty vague. Now turn this round and look at your own business. What sort of image do you think outsiders have of it? You may know what you would like them to know, but have you any idea what they actually know?

Ask the average man or woman in the street what he or she knows about dotcom business. Most of them, unless they are already dallying with the internet, will know nothing about it except that they don't want it. Umpteen years ago, they said that about colour television. Years before that, about talkies ... before that, about movies ... the list is endless.

A corporate image is based on people's knowledge and experience. This may be good, bad or indifferent. You know all about your business: outsiders know less, and probably much less about it. Unless you tell them about yourself. That is the job of PR – not to tell them how wonderful you are but what you actually are.

If you do not deserve a good image – and that is really a good reputation – you must do something about it. You may have to create a corporate identity as described in the next chapter. But it has a lot to do with how, as a business, you behave, or are seen to behave, and are capable of winning a deservedly good perceived image.

How do images come about?

Many images come about by accident. When a colleague went for an interview with a well-known company in the insecticide and pest control business, he had to call at their beautiful country house headquarters. He asked the bus conductor to drop him at this splendid mansion. The man retorted, 'Oh, you mean the rattery.' Supposing the job applicant had been a shorthand typist? It would have been a very unpleasant shock. The nickname had occurred because a laboratory was attached to the house where experiments were carried out into rat poisons.

On the other hand, a reputation or image can be gained by experience. If we travel, we all know what we think of various airlines or hotels. Marks and Spencer have gained an enviable image because of the experience of their customers, even if it takes a denting now and then with charges that they are not at the forefront of fashion any more.

Two immigrants to Australia wrote a book about life in Australia. The last words in the book were 'There's only one thing wrong with Australia – there's no Marks and Spencer'.

So, to gain a really favourable image, **you** have to do something about it, not hire a PR consultant like many politicians do in the vain hope that they can create one out of thin air. Margaret Thatcher tried that, but, according to the polls, it did not do her much good because people judged by her behaviour and their experience – if you are unemployed, a change of voice or hair style makes no difference. Cabinet Ministers and Prime Ministers since her day have also tried this route, not with huge success.

It is not suggested that business people necessarily seek to bamboozle people about their corporate image. In all sincerity, they may be complacent and believe that everyone loves them, or even knows how good they are.

There was a very large American chemical company with offices in the West End of London, and a factory in the north of England. They made some very clever additives which enhanced many products, from paper to paint. The final customer knew nothing about these additives or who made them. There was a back-selling operation to persuade specifiers to use the product. Sitting in their West End office overlooking a park, it was easy for the directors to believe they were God's gift to various industries and to millions of consumers. Their PR consultant did not share their opinion, and wanted better evidence before planning a PR programme.

So a research company was commissioned to conduct a telephone-by-appointment interview with their buyers all over the country, asking about their performance in comparison with those of half-a-dozen rival companies. The identity of the sponsor of the survey was not revealed. The results were shattering. The company had a fuddy-duddy image, partly because its sales representatives were dull technicians rather than salesmen! There was nothing wrong with the product, but it was badly presented at the point-of-sale, that is with specifiers and purchasing officers. The sales force was retrained, and a series of humorous trade press advertisements was produced, while credit for the company's achievements was sought through press relations.

Check-list

Here is a check-list of considerations which affect the corporate image, matters which may have to be dealt with very seriously before a corporate image campaign can be carried out. Indications may result from feedback such as complaints, poor tone and quality of media coverage, salespeople's reports, slow reordering, slow stock turn round and other clues, but opinion research or an image study may be necessary.

1. The after-market
It is important to consider very carefully how you treat your clients

and customers, once they have joined your flock. One of this age's most common bleats is that companies do not look after their customers once they have made the purchase of services or goods.

? How well do you look after customers once they have bought your product or service?

? Is there a reliable after-sales or spare parts service?

? Are service engineers fully trained?

? Do you issue a complicated 'small print' guarantee or warranty, or do you simply promise to refund or replace if a customer is dissatisfied or the product goes wrong?

? Are instructions and manuals easy to understand, perhaps with plenty of pictures or diagrams?

? Do you follow up customers and keep them interested?

? Do you educate customers so that they benefit fully from their purchases?

2. Is your advertising creditable?

Attitudes to advertising help the corporate image. Some companies make sure their advertising is always good for the corporate image as well as to sell the product.

Knocking copy, as we have seen in the motor-car industry and in politics, has harmed corporate images.

3. Is your web site creditable?

? Is it up-to-date, with today's news rather than yesterday's?

? Can visitors navigate easily to find what they are looking for, or do they have to flick through endless buttons?

? Do you check regularly to ensure that you have good positioning on the search engines?

? Do people keep coming back?

4. How good are your industrial relations?

A company with a bad reputation for industrial disputes is unlikely to enjoy a good reputation with employees, distributors, importers or customers. Bad management provokes many disputes, largely through lack of communications.

Even the village shop can have bad industrial relations – being too harsh on the paper-boy who turns up late, sacking a young mother because she has too much time off, arguing with delivery people. These things are noticed by the community and more so in smaller areas where everybody knows everybody else. Bad feelings are hard to break once a reputation for stinginess has been created.

5. How convenient are your packaging and delivery services?

Nowadays, the range of available packaging devices is enormous. Customers are easily put off by irritatingly strong and permanently sealed boxes, or bottle-caps that will not turn without a monkey-wrench.

? Do you concentrate on the economics or the customer convenience of your packaging? Bad relations can be created by poor packaging.

? Do you deliver when you say you will?

6. How good are your trade relations?

This is an important area of PR. The person behind the counter or on your answerline can make or break you if he or she does not fully understand your product.

7. How does the stock market treat you?

If City editors, investment analysts and others in the money market do not understand your strengths, their comments and advice could affect your share price.

You could be heading for a take-over bid!

8. How do people like your premises?

Whether it be factory, office, shop or other premises frequented by your various publics, their reactions and impressions are vital to your image.

? What impression do your premises create?

?   Would you be impressed if the premises belonged to someone else and you were the visitor?

?   When people visit your web site, do they find it visually attractive?

A garden in front of the factory, decent chairs to sit on and an efficient receptionist, a neat store layout, and even the location all make or mar your corporate image. You don't have to impress but you do have to please.

Gordon Selfridge knew this at the turn of the century when he turned shopping into a pleasant day's outing. Boots introduced the idea of laying out their goods on open counters. Even the smallest shopkeeper can make the shop more attractive to visit than those of competitors.

Web sites are just as prone to being instantly discounted as are gloomy or uninviting shop-fronts. A few moments surfing the web will reveal any number of dull and unappetising sites that do not deserve a visit, even if the subject area is of interest.

8. How do you deal with correspondence?

?   Do you answer letters the same day they are received? Few people do, and business correspondence is one of the most infuriating experiences many customers have.

A colleague recently agreed to buy an insurance policy. It took weeks to get a reply – meanwhile she received *two further sales letters* for the same offer! The impression gained was of a very inefficient company, and it was one of the biggest.

?   What is the quality of your correspondence?

?   Does the owner of that terrible signature type his name underneath?

?   Is the telephone number legible, or is it in small grey print? (This is often a fault with business cards.)

The above is a spread of all kinds of behaviour which can irritate when it is done wrong or delight when completed properly and with the customer/company relationship in mind. Unless they are perfected, it is a waste of time chasing an elusive favourable corporate image.

All these things are elementary public relations. They concern different departmental heads, but the directive needs to come from the top. People in middle management are often complacent about such matters. This narrow view needs to be broadened by PR-minded management which realises that the corporate image depends on how people judge the company by its behaviour as it affects them. In the end, everyone in a company contributes to PR, especially when they have any sort of contact with outsiders whose opinions and attitudes matter.

The corporate image becomes the sum total of hundreds, thousands and maybe millions of expressions of goodwill or ill-will. Thus, it is impossible to polish a tarnished image, only to put it right or make sure it never happens. Nor must we forget that the behaviour of top management reflects on the corporate image. This can go outside the company and include their social and maybe political life.

Business people can often contribute to the corporate image by the way in which they are seen to behave publicly, as was the case with the head of the Stagecoach company and his views expressed over the issue of Section 28, when its abolition from the Education and Local Government Act was being so hotly debated in mid-2000. The leaders of national companies need to take great care that they do not alienate large sections of their various publics if they espouse political, religious or ethnic causes, lest they lose much of their consumer base. As the phrase goes, people can easily express their opinions with their feet.

3

Do I Need a Corporate Identity?

'You can't turn vin ordinaire into Chateau Lafite by changing the label on the bottle.'

Karl Onopohl

How is your corporate identity? Do you have one? Or have you perhaps confused corporate identity with corporate image? The two are quite different. One is how an organisation is recognised physically, the other is how its character and behaviour is perceived mentally.

It all began with people who wanted others to know who they were, and maybe to frighten them. Vikings carried pictures of fearsome birds on the sails of their ships. Kings led armies into battle with crosses and eagles on their breastplates and shields.

That became a dodgy business because the other side knew who to kill first. It happened to Harold at Hastings. Imagine what would have happened if Churchill and Hitler had lead their respective armies into battle, no doubt one identified by his cigar and the other by his moustache. Many millions of people may have stayed alive. Unfortunately, the kings of old disliked the fatality rate of instant recognition, so they made their knights dress the same as themselves, and that was the birth of the uniform, a kind of camouflage for kings. Nowadays, military leaders keep themselves well out of the way of the action. They even have bomb-proof underground bunkers.

Throughout history, corporate identity schemes have been applied to ships, stage coaches, railways, buses, trams, taxicabs, delivery vans and all kinds of transportation until today it is one of the entertainments of travel to spot the identities of aircraft at the world's airports or the liveries of major hauliers. There are even hauliers fan-clubs who vie with each other over who has the best fleet, such as the supporters of the French firm Norbert Dentressangle and the Brits with their Eddie Stobart.

Today, if one walks down the High Street in search of a branch of a particular bank or shop one has no difficulty in finding it because it is identified in exactly the same way as in any other high street, including high streets abroad. Even some of the oldest forms of identification such as the inn sign, the barber's red and white pole or the apothecary's bottles of coloured liquid have survived to the present day. Some have been jollied up like the Lloyd's Bank black horse.

How well is your business identified? Do you have a common scheme of corporate identity? Do your business cards match your letterheads? Have you a simple, recognisable logo?

Not every business has a standard scheme, and it has become a very specialised business designing a distinctive corporate identity. Some companies adopt a new corporate identity, perhaps because the old one had become old-fashioned or did not represent the type of business they are now in. Some changes are more unfathomable such as BP's change in 2000 from the familiar yellow and green shield to a sunflower. Sometimes, as a result of mergers, it is necessary to create a new one.

Maybe you haven't got a scheme – only a muddle of unrelated colours, shapes and names. Different people, without asking anyone else, have ordered this or that print, advertising, design or decoration. There is no coherent instantly recognisable identification. Yet there is strength in unity, and the repeated spin-off effect of repetition. Repetition is a recognised factor in advertising, but it also applies to PR.

The corporate identity derives from the PR philosophy of creating understanding, but obviously it lends itself to every form of physical representation whether it be print, packaging, premises, web sites, vehicles, dress or advertising.

It is essential that a corporate identity is **distinctive**, **easily recognised** and **remembered** and, if possible, **characteristic**. Moreover, it can be an extensive operation, involving everything by which a company can be identified.

There are five basic components:

- **Logo** – first there is the logo which may or may not be a trade mark. This is a special design which becomes the badge of the organisation. Some very simple but effective ones have been based on the signature of the founder like Ford, Cadbury and Fokker. Others incorporate initials like ICI and ITT, usually using a certain typeface, or use symbolic shapes such as half chevrons. A clever one is the oscilloscope effect used by Plessey.

- **Colour** – which may be incorporated in packaging like the yellow Kodak box, or made very distinctive in van liveries as with British Telecom. Dark blue has been chosen by British Airways, red by Mitsubishi, green by Holiday Inn, and so on.

- **Special typeface** – this may be chosen so that all printed materials are distinguished by a particular typeface.

- **Trade character** – there are several famous ones such as the White Horse whisky horse, the Michelin man and the striding figure of Johnnie Walker.

- **Permanent slogan** – this may be associated with the corporate identity scheme, such as Bell's *'Afore Ye Go'* or BMW's *'Ultimate driving machine'*.

A corporate identity scheme may consist of all or some of these five components. They obviously strengthen advertising campaigns, and in themselves provide that essential ingredient of advertising, repetition. But advertising is only one of the uses to which the corporate identity may be put.

Agreed, it is a costly business to first of all have a corporate identity scheme designed, and even more expensive to adopt it throughout all a company's physical representations. But every item which could carry the corporate identity has to be produced, printed or painted at some time. Why not standardise them and gain from a consistent appearance? These exercises do not always go well – many will recall the expensive fiasco of BA repainting all the tailfins of their aircraft with 'ethnic' designs.

If you do not have a scheme, have you looked at what is happening throughout your business? It could be an enlightening and alarming experience. Your company could look like a woman who makes frequent changes of hair-style, make-up and dress. She lives in perpetual disguise.

Why not take a closer look? Collect examples of everything that is printed in your company's name – business cards, letterheadings, invoices, sales literature, catalogues, house journals, advertisements, annual reports. Collect them from every branch and plant. Then, collect pictures of premises, vehicles and any other form of transportation. And what about other items such as give-aways – ashtrays, pens, calendars, diaries? Then there is dress – caps, overalls, uniforms, dresses and other apparel with which staff are supplied.

A study of this collection could be a shock. They all exist. They are all necessary. Yet at various times different people have introduced their own ideas. Colours and typography or signwriting may vary, and there may be no logo, or variations on something produced years ago. It is a creative mess. It needs the discipline of a corporate identity scheme.

Once such a scheme has been finalised, the next step is to make sure that everyone responsible for buying is supplied with a manual setting out the logo (and how it should appear in colour and black and white), the stipulated colour with a colour swatch and its number (e.g. Pantone), an alphabet in the correct typeface, and replicas for all painters and decorators of transportation and premises. This can be in a ring-binder, a wallet or in the form of a poster. Everyone will be expected to comply with these instructions. Not everything can be changed at once, but gradually over a matter of months the company will become uniformly represented and portrayed.

Once there was a holding company which had about fifteen trading companies. Each had its own name and identity. But small isn't always beautiful. The managing director saw that future success lay in the powerful selling effect of size and strength. So one company name was created. This made necessary new printing, decorating, sign-writing, and advertising. It was the supreme opportunity to create a new, distinctive corporate identity to replace fifteen very haphazard and indifferent ones. One of the most striking results was that within a few months, the company became nationally visible on the roads of Britain. It was seen to be a large organisation. Yet those same vehicles, in fifteen different liveries, had been there all the time.

Unity is strength and a great morale booster. It is like showing the flag and it exudes confidence – among employees, distributors, customers and many others.

The corporate identity enhances the corporate image.

4

How do I get Media Coverage?

'News is what someone, somewhere doesn't want you to print
– all the rest is advertising.'

William Randolph Hearst

The late American newspaper magnate was a cynic. Philip Kotler has misled the marketing world with his misinterpretation of press relations as 'planting commercially significant news'. More to the point was Ivy Ledbetter Lee's dictum that all PR press material must be 'of interest and value' to the public.

You want to be read about in the press, seen on television, listened to on the radio and, more and more acceptably, found on the web. How is this possible when there are three conflicting views on PR media coverage?

The media still reflect Hearst's view, or at least they pretend to but they do have to grudgingly admit their gratitude for and sometimes their dependence on PR sources of information. Nevertheless, an adversarial situation does exist between the media and PR practitioners, mainly because neither understands the other or because their objectives are different.

The marketing world still adopts a myopic view of PR, believing it to be a dubious ally that has to be accepted at times. But only reluctantly!

The professional PR practitioner knows that unless his story is of interest and value to the reader, viewer, listener or web browser, it will not be accepted by the editor or producer. If he deviates from this he is a menace to PR. A lot of news release writers are.

But where do you stand as the business person who wants to be in the news? A foot in either or neither camp?

Do you think you have some democratic right to be published or broadcast? A great many business people do, as if the media belong to them as a public service to which they are entitled. They tell their PROs or PR consultants 'I want this in the Financial Times tomorrow morning', when the story is of no interest to anyone else beyond themselves. They approve, and even have the temerity to re-write professionally written news releases, to say what they want to say, not what people may care to read.

The only way to achieve media coverage is to give the media what it wants, how and when it wants it. Then, because the story is used, you get what you want in the end. It won't work the other way round. As a business person you need to understand that the media are businesses too. Their purpose is to make money. They are not charities. It was the late Lord Thomson who, without being a cynic, said that his acquisition of Scottish Television was 'a licence to print money'. He meant it. Even the BBC has to compete with ITV. One day it may even have to rely on advertising or sponsorship.

On the whole, in Britain, the media provide entertainment, and even the news has to be entertainment whether it be about exciting events or because news readers are attractive and wear attractive clothes. It is no accident that the biggest circulation newspapers and magazines, and the TV programmes with the largest audience figures, are the ones which are most entertaining.

An apparently serious press, radio or TV interview will be more entertaining if the interview can be provocative. The Sun has the biggest sales and readership of any British newspaper, and BBC's EastEnders and ITV's Coronation Street have the biggest TV audiences.

The newspapers are inundated with material from their own staff, news agencies, special correspondents and contributors, plus PR sources. Much of this can appear only on certain pages, in particular features or columns, or on special days. As a result, a great deal of what they receive has to be discarded. Most of the material from PR sources is unpublishable, mainly because it is of 'interest and value' only to the sender.

If you want media coverage, your story must be news which reaches the right editors at the right time, is capable of competing with the work of professional journalists, and does not commit the faults of the majority of rejected news releases.

Surprised? Dejected? You don't have to be. It is perfectly easy to write a publishable news release, and reasonably easy to get it published. Not many news releases are publishable, so very few of them ever get published. The main culprit is someone in authority who insists on destroying releases before they are ever despatched. ***This could be you!*** It would save a lot of time and money if PROs or PR consultants put these uselessly 'approved' stories in their own waste bins instead of putting editors to the trouble of filling theirs.

Did it ever occur to you that the average editor, confronted by hundreds of news releases every morning, has only one second in which to decide whether each one is of any use to him? That was stated by a Fleet Street news editor. Editors do not sit there poring over every word, and every page of long-winded news releases. And with direct access from the computer, bad news releases are going to be even less popular and will be instantly walloped with the 'delete' button.

The reason why so many news releases are bad is that they in no way resemble the news reports which are printed in the press. The easiest way to learn how to write a news release, or how to approve a news release draft because it is publishable, is to read and analyse what actually appears in editorial columns. Journalists the world over are not very original and they all rather monotonously yet logically follow the same pattern of presentation. Very few news releases do this. Writing news releases is the worst-done craft in the business, but in the hope that the writers are actually more professional than they appear to be, one can only assume that superiors mutilate their work. In studying the press, the first thing you will notice is that each publication has its own headline for the same story. Headlines are written for certain very definite reasons, which makes it silly to give a news release a clever catchy headline as if it were an advertisement. Printed headlines are specially written, often by specialist headline writers, to be different, competitive, characteristic or to fit the space.

➔ The *headline* of a news release should simply state what the story is about, which is helpful to the editor.

➔ The next, and perhaps most important thing, that you will notice is that the *subject* is stated in the first few words of the first sentence of the first paragraph.

Sounds reasonable, doesn't it? After all, it's what the reader wants to know, what you as a reader want to know.

But what happens? What do you insist on? What do you think is the subject, the most important thing in the story? To you, the most important thing is you, or rather your company. But this is rarely the subject, is it? The subject is what your company has done or is going to do. In other words, the opening words *should* say:

'A new fireproof fabric has been created by the Fireproof Fabric Company.'

and not

'The Fireproof Fabric Company have created a new fireproof fabric.'

That is lesson number one. It's the crunch.

If you study the average printed news report more closely, you will find that the first paragraph is a summary or digest of the whole story. In fact, if you went quickly through a newspaper reading only the first paragraph of each story you would have a complete digest of the entire contents.

The journalistic trick is to blow the whole story in the first paragraph, and then go on and develop it. In the case of a news release, the first paragraph may be all the editor has space for, but you are home and dry because the essence of the story has been published. So, when you are next approving the draft of a news release, check that the subject is in the first few words – not the company name – and that the opening paragraph tells it all in a nutshell.

Some attention has been given to the news release because it is the most common form of press relations, the one worst done, and the one which provokes the greatest criticism by the media. If you want to succeed in gaining media coverage, getting the news release right is the first step. This applies equally to releases sent by traditional methods or those obtainable on the internet. See also chapter 6.

There are certain writing and presentation styles which are important but let's deal with the most common fault in the content of the news release. It is ***puffery***. Puffery is what editors call advertising. Most of them hate advertising.

Journalism and copywriting are two different kinds of writing. When a news release errs from journalism and verges on copywriting, editors are immediately hostile. They do not permit free advertisements in their columns. Puffery not only includes plugs, promotional language, and emotive language but self-praise, however justified this may seem to the writer.

A news release should be objective and factual, avoiding any superlatives or comment. You may not agree with this if you believe your company is the largest or the brand leader or the product is the finest of its kind. But it is not your place to say so. Remember, anything that is printed will appear as if written by a staff writer. It will be the journal's story, not yours. Consequently, it needs to be written as if a journalist had written it, given the same facts.

This may be difficult to swallow. You may feel entitled to be enthusiastic, but the newspaper is not going to express your enthusiasm, only the bare, unadorned facts. A news release should be as unemotional, and as non-promotional as an instruction on how to wire an electric plug. If a release is written like this, it may be published without alteration. A journalist may even put his own name to it, an honour indeed.

But some editors will insist on having the story re-written, and that is where mistakes occur. The best way to avoid such mistakes occurring is to write short sentences and short paragraphs which are difficult to get wrong even if paraphrased.

The news release is not the only way to get media coverage, but similar considerations apply whether it be a feature article, a press reception, an interview or a broadcast. There must be no advertising, the information given must be factual, it must be newsworthy, and it must be of interest and value to the reader, viewer or listener.

In other words, you have to put yourself in the place of your audience. What would interest you if you were the reader? Not, what do you want to tell the reader?

5

How do I Deal with Reporters and Interviewers?

'I do not resent criticism, even when, for the sake of emphasis, it parts for the time from reality.'
Winston Churchill, House of Commons, January 22, 1941

A journalist rings up and asks if he can interview you. Or you are invited to the studio for a radio or television interview. How do you react? Do you panic? Are you flattered? What do you expect and what do you do about it?

Your reactions will depend on how you understand each medium, and the press, radio and television have their own characteristics. Let's begin with the press.

In Britain, according to BRAD, there are some 12,000 publications. Roughly, they fall into the categories of national newspapers, regional newspapers, free newspapers, special interest magazines, trade, technical and professional magazines, and year books and directories. They differ according to their frequency, target readership and printing process.

National newspapers serve certain social grades, which tends to be peculiar to class-conscious Britain. The social grades are based on occupation, not income. Recognising these distinctions will help to understand the approach of a journalist from one of these newspapers. The following table is a rough breakdown although obviously there are people who read more than one class of newspaper. A person who has the Daily Express delivered at home may well read the Financial Times at the office. The Sunday Times has an A-B readership.

	Social grade		Newspapers
A	Upper middle class, business, political, social leaders	3%	The Times, The Financial Times, Sunday Times
B	Liberal-intellectual teacher	13%	The Guardian, The Observer, The Daily Telegraph, The Independent, The Sunday Independent, The Sunday Telegraph
C1	Lower middle class, white-collar, white-blouse office workers etc.	22%	The Daily Express, The Daily Mail, The Sunday Express, The Mail on Sunday
C2	Skilled working class	32%	The Daily Mirror, The Sun, The Star, The Sunday People, The News of the World, The Sunday Mirror
D	Semi-skilled working class	20%	
E	Others, e.g. pensioners	9%	

Circulations are in ascending order from top to bottom, e.g. around 800,000 for The Times and around 4,000,000 for The Sun.

Thus, the questions a journalist may ask will be determined by the class interests of his or her readers, and the nature and content of interviews will vary accordingly. The business person needs to be aware of these variations, and be prepared with relevant information and answers. One journalist may be interested in the company's financial prospects, another in its export record and yet another in its industrial relations or its attitudes to women or immigrant labour. It will pay to study in advance a copy of the newspaper which the visiting journalist represents.

In a similar way, the industry may have several trade journals but their editorial policies and target readerships may be very different. So, now – **think enemy!**

By that remark, it is not suggested that a journalist should be received antagonistically, but it may be a safe tactic to remember that he does represent a point of view different from yours.

Journalists are usually in a hurry, and this may be inconvenient to you. Again, there is a contrast in needs. Your product goes on for ever, but a newspaper is a new product every day. Had you ever thought of this? If the journalist does not get his story back to his editor by a certain hour this morning, it will be too late this afternoon, and useless tonight – let alone tomorrow.

A weekly magazine may have only two days in which to complete the interview, and a monthly magazine only two weeks (and probably many weeks before actual publication). The lead times laid down by editing, production, printing and distribution procedures need to be appreciated, however inconvenient this may be to you.

You may well find that the person who calls you is a freelance journalist, with ties maybe to several publications and a greater specialist knowledge than the one-paper generalist. This can be to your advantage, allowing you to promote your material to a wider readership. Likewise, news agencies can spread information more widely. It is to your advantage to find out how these journalists work and how they can work for you.

Sometimes, the interview may be no more than a telephone call, and you may recall the furore that arose some years ago over a garbled telephone interview between a journalist and a Palace spokesman over relations between Mrs Thatcher and the Queen.

There is also a difference between what you would like to tell the world, and the kind of story the journal publishes. Be careful! The old adage 'good news is bad news' is unfortunately very true of the media, but this is not the fault of the media. It's what sells newspapers. It's a perverted form of entertainment, if you like. If things are going well, it is not that interesting and it is no more than people expect. But if something goes wrong, that is unusual, dramatic and newsworthy.

One of the most successful news stories ever was Watergate in 1972. And how the British press keep looking for another Watergate over here!

The idea of 'something-gate' is now very strong and has reached the dictionaries as a phrase meaning a substantial scandal, such was the strength of the events around the original '-gate'. It happened again over Reagan and the Iranian/Nicaraguan arms scandal (which the press dubbed 'Irangate') and even hit some papers in Bill

Clinton's time as 'Lewinskigate'.. What you do not want to read is the story of 'you-gate' or 'your-company-gate'!

So why has that journalist asked to see you? Is it to find something dramatic to write about? Have you got a weak spot, are you vulnerable? It's no use refusing to see him or her. 'No comment' is the worst of all answers. And it's useless expecting your PRO or PR consultant to stand in for you because that is just what journalists expect. If you are a one-person business, then it has to be you who meets the press head-on. At the same time, this means that you have no other recourse if it goes badly – no one to blame but yourself – so you had better be careful.

Remember it is difficult to make friends of journalists. It is dangerous to give 'off-the-record' confidential insights because it is difficult, afterwards, for a journalist to recall what was 'on' and what was 'off' the record. It is best to stick to telling journalists what you are willing to have printed. Even that will not prevent them putting their own interpretation and embellishments on what you say or don't say! The 'spin doctor' may be a recently invented phrase, but the concept has been around since news was first scratched on the walls of the cave.

Don't fudge issues. Always have some answer ready. But don't be like some politicians and ignore questions by being so articulate that you virtually create your own questions and impose your own answers. This will only antagonise interviewers and prejudice being invited again.

Interviews at your place

With these cautionary provisions – which are not intended to condemn journalists but rather to establish their naturally different standpoint – let's consider the interview itself.

Like the Boy Scout, be prepared.

- Make sure you know your facts so that you can talk easily and confidently.
- Do your homework.

- Be articulate, as this shows confidence.
- You should be the king in your own castle.
- Welcome journalists courteously. Thank them for coming. Offer them refreshment. Give them a comfortable chair. Do this, even if you think they are a cross between detectives and doctors, unwelcome interrogators.
- You are the host. It's your office. They are your guests. So, stay in command!

You are not obliged to see them, and whatever the claptrap about freedom of the press, and the right of the public to know, they represent a profit-making business just as you do. You have a perfect right to tell them to go to hell – except that it is a wiser tactic to do what they ask as far as you can.

It is also worth remembering that unless your journalist is a specialist writer, he or she probably has no technical knowledge of your business. Most journalists have to write about countless topics and can be expert in none. Their expertise lies in probing for an angle which will make the story interesting for their readers.

Your visitor may have been given an angle by the editor such as 'find out how many people will be made redundant by this new policy' or 'is it true that the company plans to buy components from Indonesia?' They might be very sensitive topics. He may be looking for a scoop, and it is unwise to favour one newspaper.

But in particular, remember how little journalists may know about your business. You may have to educate them and, in so doing, you must not confuse them with technicalities which they could get wrong. Without being contemptuous or condescending, you may have to talk in one-syllable language which makes the subject easy to understand. It may help if you take journalists round the plant, offices or the laboratory, and let them see things at first hand and ask questions of people.

Interviews in the studio

In a studio interview for radio or television, the roles are reversed, you are the guest and the interviewer is in command. You have to be more guarded in your replies, but still well-informed and articulate. He is looking for the main chance to provoke you into saying something, perhaps unintentionally, which will give zest to the programme.

The studio environment is different from your familiar office. You are isolated. You have no handy telephone, or secretary in the outer office if you need to call for information. You are far more vulnerable – the fly in the spider's web.

The interviewer can be hostile. He or she may seem to be hostile simply because – especially if it is a live broadcast – time is limited and questions will be fired more urgently than in the more leisurely circumstances of an interview in your office. Curt, rapid-fire questions are not therefore rude or badgering, and the reason for them needs to be understood, otherwise you could take offence. If you then behaved like a wounded bull elephant, the interview would be disastrous for you.

The radio studio can be a bleak little place. It is likely to be a small room with just you and the interviewer and a microphone or tape recorder on the table between you. An engineer will be working mysteriously behind a glass panel. Very informal, like a conversation.

- How do you sound?
- Can you speak slowly, confidently, in a warm attractive voice?
- Can you chuckle?
- Can you sound as if you are enjoying the broadcast, and communicating with the audience?

Not easy. Not everyone has a charismatic voice, although a regional accent may help to lend music to a voice. Practice making your voice rise and fall, otherwise it will sound very monotonous.

A television studio is larger and busier with hot bright lights and cameras and technicians moving about. You may have to rehearse. You may have to wear make-up. There can be many distractions, and you need to settle yourself comfortably in your chair, relax and concentrate on the interviewer.

Don't look at the camera. If the producer wants a full-face picture he will instruct the cameraman over the headphones. Be careful to control irritating mannerisms like scratching your nose, removing your glasses and putting them on again, or buttoning and unbuttoning your jacket. Try to feel at home. Watch interviews on television and see how people behave.

How do you look? Remember, people will be looking at you on a small screen in their own homes. They can be very critical of what they see. Dress appropriately, but don't wear a white shirt. Remember, the picture is in colour, and colours such as red, orange and yellow are rare. A touch of red may help, such as a red tie. People will notice what you are wearing. But don't dress outlandishly, if that is out of character. Politicians seem to have special suits, shirts and ties for television, as you may have noticed. Watch what people wear, how they look on the screen.

It is astonishing how viewers observe things they would not notice in press pictures. Celebrities who appear regularly on the box are seen to get balder, greyer, thinner, fatter or just older. Business personalities can suffer from the same critical appraisal. Do they look too young or too old for the job? Have they got crafty eyes or too tight a mouth? Would people want to work for them, or invest in their company, or even buy their goods?

Radio interviews can also be pre-recorded, either in the studio or a radio station, or by an outside radio journalist. There are also companies like Universal News Service, which will set up interviews for a fee and distribute tapes to local radio stations. If you are interested in export markets, the Central Office of Information has a studio for taping interviews which are sent to overseas radio stations.

There are also television documentaries which include a number of pre-recorded interviews. There are certain hazards in this and, if possible, when you are invited to participate in such a programme ask the producer to explain the theme of the programme and tell you the identities of other people being interviewed. Although your interview may last several minutes, and you may be under the impression that the whole interview will be screened as it took place, this does not always happen. The various interviews may be so edited that what you say on a particular point may be contrasted with what someone else says. The presenter may also comment on your remarks, even though he was not present at the original interview. What you said may be presented out of context, and the final result on screen may be very different from what you expected!

But you don't have to be interviewed on television if you don't want to. It may be wise to ask whether the audience is right for you. Are you likely to be able to say anything of value to your business, or are you merely making yourself the fall guy for an interviewer or presenter who wants to entertain his audience and build his own reputation as a television personality? Television can crucify people. Some people are so anxious to get 'on the box' and impress their friends that they end up making fools of themselves.

Broadcasting is supposed to be about informing, educating and entertaining, but it seldom extends beyond the latter, even in supposedly serious programmes. It may pay to say 'No' to invitations to appear on television. You have to ask yourself, what have you got which will contribute to the high audience ratings craved by advertisers? Probably nothing, or your contribution will not be to your advantage. The chances are that what you would like to say is of no interest to anyone except you!

However, these warnings apart, there are many opportunities for securing excellent media coverage on television, provided the subject is of interest and value to a large enough section of the audience. The business person can initiate this coverage, and does not have to be invited but can put forward his or her own ideas to the appropriate programme producer.

To do this, he needs to study what is transmitted, and read the Radio Times and TV Times to see what programmes are being presented and by whom. In doing so, he should be aware that some programmes aired by his regional station have been made by another TV station. Some programmes are networked. He may have to approach a TV company in another part of the country.

Some programmes have to be made days, weeks and maybe months ahead, such as the holiday programmes shown in January which have to be shot during the previous summer.

If you have opened a new factory, gained a big export order or invented something new, this could make a news item for your regional news bulletin. Personality stories may also be acceptable, such as your activities on behalf of a local charity, or your presentation at a conference. If you have legitimate news items like these, contact the news editor with an outline of your story.

Because it is your story, and you have the facts, the interviewer is more likely to invite you to give the facts rather than fire a barrage of less favourable questions as may occur in the more controversial interviews already described. The roles are reversed in your favour because you have a success story to tell. Success can also be unusual, dramatic and entertaining, and so suit the medium.

For more information on dealing with interviews, read 'How To Handle Media Interviews' by Andrew Boyd, Management Books 2000, 1999.

6

How Can I Develop e-PR?

"Tis true; there's magic in the web of it."
William Shakespeare (Othello)

Some of the statistics about the internet are astonishing, especially where e-commerce is concerned. The new technologies are being used to great effect and the number of people with global access is increasing daily. In the UK alone in mid-2000, there were some 10 million people online, with about 10% of those claiming to be online regularly. A survey by Nua Internet Surveys in February 2000 showed a world total of people online as 275 million, and increasing rapidly.

When you consider that, theoretically at least, they all have access to your web site, then the potential for effective e-PR is colossal. Does that differ from non-e PR? Not one whit – the principles are just the same although the dimensions and techniques may vary slightly.

On a word of caution, the internet seems to represent the change-over point from traditional to progressive views about the world, life and everything. To many people who have grown up into their commercial and social patterns without the net, it is a mysterious place to be avoided if possible. To an ever increasing (and probably younger) group, it represents the new way forward, the inevitable and totally acceptable face of progress. It will take a generation to balance out and meanwhile, PR people have to challenge and change those traditional views. The internet will therefore have two main elements of PR activity – first to promote your own business to the world at large. This chapter looks at some ways of doing this. Second, it is your way of finding out what your competitors, your detractors, your fans and your industry at large are doing – right now, right here and in view of everyone else. That is a critical point – what you show on your piece of the internet is on view to the world. It had better be good!

That the PR industry takes the internet seriously is not in contention. In 2000, the IPR and the PRCA formed a joint Internet Commission with the long-term aims of providing qualified PR practitioners with access to and an understanding of the internet and IT in general for the advancement of PR practice. Following an early report that showed how the internet was forcing a radical change on the way PR practitioners worked, the Commission set itself a target to be 'the world's best place to undertake PR electronically by the year 2002'.

Some writers estimate that by the year 2020, **all** businesses will use the internet and it will be accessed by around 80% of all homes world-wide. A huge amount of trade will take place and you need to be there, up and running with a firm PR policy built into your e-activities. Now is the time to get in, not 'well, maybe we will look at it next year.' Seize the moment – 'carpe diem' as they say, or perhaps that should be 'carpe cyber-diem' to mix classical languages.

For the purposes of this chapter, we need to assume that you are already on the web, with your own site established or at least to the forefront of your planning. For a comprehensive view of the essential aspects of e-commerce and the way to set it all up, read 'The Secrets of Profitable E-commerce' by Laurel Alexander, Management Books 2000, 2000.

Web site

As your web site is the electronic identity and shop-front of your company, there are a number of aspects that need clarifying. It is where your customers may first come across you, so you need to be able to say, 'Come in and welcome'.

Start with your e-name, your domain name. The points made in Chapter 2 about names apply equally to your domain name. Ideally it should identify you instantly and clearly. www.fred-fernackerpans. co.uk may be fine for Fred himself, but it does not tell potential customers why they should visit the site. Whereas www.fredwindowclean.co.uk does. Some of the cleverest names are short and to the point – they generally reflect a long-term acceptance of the name by the public, before the advent of the internet.

Most of the best short names have been registered now, but the introduction of new sets of top-level domain names such as .firm, .info, .store and so on will ease the situation. From a PR point of view, a top level domain (one ending in .co.uk, .com, .org etc.) is essential to present the company as sufficiently serious about e-commerce. The use of a domain which incorporates the ISP (Internet Service Provider) name is for the small players and private domains – names such as www.fredwindowclean@ cheaponet.net.

There are two main essentials with all web sites – the visitor needs **information** and the site needs to encourage **interactivity.** Over-riding these two necessities is one general principle – the site must be good, it must be the bee's knees.

When putting together the site, be BOLD, be contentious, be dynamic, be vigorous, be full of pizzazz, dare to be different. You want people to visit – they will not prowl around sites that are dull as ditch-water or those which have no zap or oomph! You have been warned.

Information

In order to develop the mutual understanding that is PR, the information on your site needs to be relevant, current and interesting. People surfing or even deliberately seeking the type of information you offer will not stay and read if the material is poor or partial. There is no advantage in merely dropping your snail-mail brochure into your site – what is required is a different animal.

What needs to be there to achieve your objectives? Generally the layout will be different from standard brochures – there is not so much choice of space, format and size, for instance, being stuck with a standard VDU screen shape, quite a lot of which is taken up with banner headings and the like. Ideally the blocks of text should be limited to no more that a few hundred words – say 400/500 at most. You should include the following.

- Company and product information – make it grab the attention. Avoid excessive self-praise, but make the text relevant to readers and succinct and to the point.

- A question and answer section is useful – you can include prepared answers to FAQs (frequently asked questions – an acronym that you will often find on web sites).

- Suggestions and favourite topics – these can be additional pages accessed from your home page. Include a few short pieces about the successes some of your customers have enjoyed with you.

More about what to put in later in this chapter. Let people know about your business and how it can help them. Inform, entertain, persuade, amuse even – but do not badger, cajole or threaten because people will zap off elsewhere very rapidly and you will have lost the initiative.

Too many sites are over fussy and crammed with bits of this and bits of that. Always bear in mind that people want to find their way around the site quickly – it must be easily navigated – so use straight forward instructions and easily understood language. It is like entering a store – customers do not want to be confused by a welter of garish signage and perplexing and unclear displays. You want the visitors (to both shop and site) to leave eventually feeling that they have been well treated and that their expectations were fulfilled. That way, your reputation will spread and people will start to talk about you favourably.

Interaction

The internet is a magnificent source of opportunities to interact with other people, whether they are private individuals or other traders and companies like yours. Totally unlike traditional methods of publicising your company, with the internet, you can receive immediate reactions to your site and its content and can respond. How you interact will affect your reputation for better or worse. This does presuppose that you have carefully designed your site to excite reaction – we will look at some aspects of site design later on.

The most successful web sites are very interactive – people can express their opinions and reactions which they cannot do with newspaper articles or billboards (well, not as effectively!). This is even more so if you build in some characteristics to encourage interaction.

- If you sell over the internet, then clearly people will interact with you – they will need to leave a range of messages about what they want, how they are willing to pay for it, where it should be sent and so on. This gives you a variety of opportunities to respond and thereby improve your image and reputation. Speak about the benefits of your products. Send additional material that will encourage your customers to stay with you.

- Giving away something for free – especially if it will actually benefit the customer – is a powerful way of cementing the supplier-customer relationship. Everyone likes a freebie and people do talk to others about good service and extra service that they have received.

- A number of computer programs are available which will allow you to ask for and receive customer feedback – or indeed feedback from journalists who have received your press releases. There is also a feeling of openness about a firm which invites comments, whether they be critical or adulatory. You do need to follow up any comments that demand a response – either by direct personal contact or through the news page on your web site. Listen to customers and act accordingly.

- Online auctions are increasing in number – you could consider this idea. It does encourage contact with your site and allows you to build up a sizeable mailing list as well as being able to offer a degree of expectation and excitement as the auction progresses.

- Competitions appeal to many people and can be easily organised on your site. Make sure that the prizes are worth having and that the value of the prize will encourage enough people to enter to make the exercise financially viable. Again, people will talk about successful competitions.

● Discussion groups are popular – there are tens of thousands of discussion groups worldwide, catering for every conceivable interest. You can join an existing group, but do be careful to observe the rules of netiquette – you will not be allowed to flagrantly flaunt your company or products but you will be allowed, even encouraged, to contribute to debates and e-conversations about topics of interest. This will permit you to promote your involvement in important issues and ideas of the day. Join a group quietly at first – don't leap in with both feet. See how it works and, in time, you can progress to taking a leading role within the group – a useful PR exercise.

Image and identity

In chapter 2, we looked at corporate image and in Chapter 3 at corporate identity. On the web, image and identity are equally as important – in some ways, even more important, because web browsers can flip into your site and out again far more quickly, for example, than a pedestrian can walk past your shop. Few people will read every word on your site just as people do not wander through every department in a store or read every page in a thick catalogue.

What is needed is something that will attract and retain interest. Browsers must recognise who you are and what you do within a few seconds of arriving at www.youroutfit.com. If you already have a good reputation and are a well-known face in your industry, then the site must echo those facts. But you are probably approaching a new audience and they can be fickle.

Not only from a trading point of view, but also as seen within a PR context, your web site must look good. The design must be good, and this is not something that an amateur can knock up in an evening. A number of programs are available to help with effective web design – Adobe Pagemill, Sausage Software's HotDog, HotMetal Pro or Dreamweaver are examples. Specialist firms offering to design and host your site are legion – choose with caution.

Remember that you will need a minimum of a Pentium 200 PC, with at least 32MB of RAM and a hard disk of at least 1Gb as well as a 28,800bps modem. Web sites are not just pretty pages of images and text. There are computer language conventions to make the systems work and other constraints that the design programs will point up.

There is also a duty on the compiler to see that the text is legal, non-offensive and non-libellous.

To create a good impression and to encourage people to stay and later on return to your site, there are a number of factors to consider.

☑ Immediate impressions – as in any interaction, first impressions are critical. The site must look good and inviting. It must not look dull and potentially boring. A quick surf through the web will show up any number of both types. (The same surf will also show up a number of web site compilers who have not grasped the essentials of English language, spelling, grammar and word choice!)

☑ Use colour wisely and illustration in a purposeful way rather than just to titillate.

☑ It is important that information from your site will download quickly. Visitors will not want to sit idly by watching their computer churn its way through endless complex images. They will go elsewhere.

☑ If you do use images, keep them small and store them as highly compressed files.

☑ Your site should (or could) include:
  ● an overall mission statement
  ● details of products or services, together with price lists if appropriate
  ● secure means of ordering (a number of systems are available to ensure security)
  ● compact, relevant and informative material that is easily read
  ● information about key personnel and company locations
  ● good links to other sites or other parts of your own site
  ● publicity about awards, testimonials and 'good works' such as

community involvements and sponsorships
- frequently asked questions (FAQs)
- memberships or registration offers
- competitions, quizzes or other entertaining items
- some form of feedback.

☒ Your site should not include:
- masses of flashing lights, twiddly bits and unnecessary fancy graphics
- curious backgrounds that render the text almost impossible to read
- a lead page that merely shows your logo or company name – the chances are that this will take ages to download when the punter wants swift information
- unclear links or other devices that the viewer may not recognise.

In Laurel Alexander's book, she offers a number of tips to wannabe web designers – keep it interactive, relevant, organised, fast, tidy, linked, focused, interesting, changing and keep on promoting it and giving away information.

What about the bad times?

All this presupposes that things are going well with you, but what happens when the jelly hits the fan? There will be occasions when your best laid plans do gang aft agley, as Robbie Burns would have put it. Then you will need to use your web site to take corrective or recuperative action. In chapter 20, we talk about dealing with a crisis and the web can be a powerful tool in that battle. You may care to look at that chapter before reading these notes.

First of all, it is necessary to lay down some plans to forestall possible crises and to train your IT staff and others to deal with such events should they occur. The first is easier said than done but the second can be achieved with forethought.

Your web site will very likely be visited by more people after a setback, partly out of morbid curiosity and partly to see how you cope with major difficulty. You have an excellent opportunity to do some creative and positive PR here. Think carefully how you need to minimise the effect of the disaster without being either cocky or dismissive. Choose your words for the site with caution and with an eye to the possible spin that people will put on them. Present evidence that you are coping well and that you appreciate all the support that you are getting from your publics (even if you are not).

Your response needs to be swift and accurate. This can be achieved either by taking the bull by the horns and posting your views and ideas directly on your web site and clearly labelling them, or by composing a simple but focused e-mail and sending it out to named people who can help to restore your reputation or good status.

It is a matter of making yourself trustable very quickly. A few days after the Concorde crash in Paris in July 2000, the media were keen to report that passengers on the Concorde flights that left London the next day were apprehensive, rather wary and very glad to land. This made better copy than reporting that many passengers still had absolute confidence in the airplane and found the flight quite unexceptional. That is the way of the media. It gave BA and Air France a greater problem of confidence re-building.

Some disgruntled customers may decide to set up a site that deliberately mimics yours and is designed to be disruptive of your trade and reputation. You may not find out about these sites straightaway – the originators may choose not to tell you about them! – and they may fester away for some time, encouraging adverse reactions and generating much heat against you.

Other people may choose to rant and rail against you via a discussion group or chatline. Again, you may not find out about this immediately. In both cases, once you have discovered these goings-on, you need to act quickly to scotch such ideas and counteract the bad vibes that there may be.

Similarly, once bad messages have been put on the web, they are likely to stay there for some time and that can perpetuate the damage until something is done to remove the items.

As chapter 20 suggests, there is mileage in thinking through what would need to be done from an internet perspective, if that jelly did hit the fan. A plan needs to be drawn up and people appointed who know how to deal with the media and how to create brilliant and effective copy for the web.

Press releases

Press releases can be done via the internet – either direct to named recipients by e-mail or posted on your web site for anyone to read and use. There are a few recommendations on press releases that will make them more likely to be noticed and more readily useable.

- Start with a bold heading – FOR IMMEDIATE RELEASE – and remember to add a date as journalists will not necessarily see the piece on the day of issue. The use of embargoes on the net is not so clever as anyone can read your message, regardless of their ethical standpoint. When using embargoes in traditional press releases, you can at least expect that the recipients will heed the warning for fear of sanctions. No so with the net.

- Choose an eyecatching headline – short, relevant, truthful and to the point.

- Keep the size down to a maximum of 500 words – some e-mail systems restrict the amount of material that can be downloaded and you do not want recipients to find that your lengthy masterpiece is chopped off in mid-sentence.

- Include your web address (URL) for future contact and a phone number for those people who wish to receive your information by non-e methods.

- On a point of style, use a simple font such as Arial and avoid blocks of capital letters. The simpler the style, the more likely it is to be downloaded without glitches – and swiftly.

- Have additional material such as reports, photographs and charts available to those who wish to see them, elsewhere on your site. Avoid adding attachments to a press release – not everyone will have the same systems as yours and they can be lost.

Other principles about press releases are covered elsewhere in this book – heed them and apply them to e-releases for good results.

Using e-mail as a PR tool

Earlier, we discussed the principles of compiling a press release for the web. The same points are essential for any e-mail, especially one designed to help the PR effort.

As with any mailing, an e-mail publicity release can be sent either to named individuals or globally to a whole raft of people who will all receive the same text and greeting. The options are as follows:

- the e-mail is addressed to individuals, who each receive a personally addressed item with no mention of any copies going elsewhere
- the e-mail is sent to individuals on a list, so that all know who else has received it
- the e-mail is posted on the web so that anyone who wants to can download it
- the e-mail is available to be sent by autoresponder to anyone who logs in

The joy of this system is of course that the message can be accessed swiftly, cheaply, efficiently, identically and in an environmentally sound fashion – no trees being chopped down or fuel used except for a minute bit of electricity. Also, the message can be updated by the minute if need be.

A disadvantage of the system, which is shared by traditional means of messaging (how much longer can we use the phrase 'traditional means' without including the concept of 'electronically'?) is that the lists of addressees must be kept up to date.

Signature files

A final point concerns the use of signature files. These are simple messages that conclude all your e-mails. They should be a maximum of four lines, no more than 70 characters wide (to avoid being chopped short), with just the company (or personal) name, contact points and addresses and a very short message about the company service or product. Programs are available which place the signature at the end of every message, automatically.

The advantage of signature files is that they are seen by every e-mail recipient every time one of your e-mails is received. They can also be clipped on the end of messages that you send to discussion groups and so on. This keeps your names and concepts in mind, whatever the message in the actual e-mail, and can be a useful and legitimate way of promoting your key purpose.

Whatever business you are in, you cannot afford to ignore the internet. It is here to stay and those people who have at least an elementary grasp of its intricacies will be in with a chance. You owe it to yourself and your company to learn how to manage your web presence and make it creative and effective in increasing your public's understanding.

It is a new tool – learn how to wield it.

7

Is sponsorship worthwhile?

'A wise man will make more opportunities than he finds.'
                                                    Francis Bacon

Why do you think companies spend money on sponsorship? Are they just being generous? Is it 'conscience' money? Why do so many companies indulge in sponsorship?

If you have never been involved in sponsorship you may doubt its value to you, or even that it is of any great value to the sponsors you hear about every day. Maybe you see it only as a form of advertising. It can be a form of advertising, or part of a marketing strategy, but it can be a PR tactic. In some cases the objectives may embrace all three.

The point is that it is very rare nowadays that anyone engages in sponsorship for purely philanthropic reasons. That was all right a long time ago when artists and composers were sponsored by wealthy patrons. There are a few very successful companies which see sponsorship as a means of putting something back into society, but most sponsorships are hard-headed business deals aimed at a definite return.

Some orchestras and ballet companies are sponsored to a degree, but even here, there is a sound financial reason for the effort and cash put in. The target of such sponsorship is partly philanthropic, but also to attract custom from the types of people who attend the sponsored performances. A number of provincial theatres put on performances that are assisted by local companies for the same reasons. Check out your local paper's entertainments page to see who is doing what.

If you are interested in sponsorship – and it could range from funding a major sports event to donating a trophy at the local flower show – four considerations have to be satisfied. These are:

- Why sponsor?
- What should you sponsor?
- What are the total costs involved?
- How can the sponsorship be organised?

Why sponsor?

You should be clear about why you want to sponsor. Here are some practical reasons:

☑ You want to enter a **new segment of the market**, but you are unknown or little known to those prospective new buyers. Yardley, previously known only for women's perfumes, used motor-racing to position itself in the market for men's toiletries. Cornhill chose test cricket to reach a household market beyond that which bought such insurance through brokers. Both were successful.

☑ You want to **increase familiarity with your name**, which is one of the reasons why Japanese companies have used sponsorship in many parts of the world. Remember, one of the strengths of sponsorship is the repetition of the name before, during and after an event. Your name becomes attached to a well-known event or prize. This can happen in a small or a big way according to whether the subject of the sponsorship is local, national or international. Sponsorship can be in aid of local branches of a large organisation such as those of a chain store or a building society, or for a product sold world-wide like Marlboro cigarettes or Kodak films.

☑ You want to **improve customer relations**, an example being the Midland Bank's sponsoring of promenade operas at Covent Garden.

☑ You may want to **enhance your corporate image** by establishing who you are and what you do.

☑ You may want to **show how your products perform** under endurance tests such as motor sports of various kinds. In the event of success, you can then boast that your product was used by the winner of the motor race, rally or safari, or it has been to the moon or 80 fathoms under the sea – in addition to the incidental publicity which will be gained during the event.

☑ You may want to **circumvent bans on advertising** – a controversial issue – which has involved firms as different as contraceptive and cigarette manufacturers.

☑ You quite frankly want **maximum media coverage** to support your overall PR campaign.

☑ You need to make your company, product or service known in **export markets.**

☑ You want to **support your distributors**, and maybe extend distribution, by popularising your product through sponsorship.

☑ You may want to **increase goodwill** by showing that your company supports worthy causes.

These are ten possible objectives, and a number may be combined.

☑ Finally, you may want to sponsor in order to be able to **offer hospitality** to business guests. This could range from giving free tickets to customers to hosting a party to watch the event. One company chairman owns a racehorse and staff parties are taken to the races when the horse is running at a nearby race course. Multi-nationals or international marketing companies gain global coverage when they support something like Grand Prix motor racing which is held at circuits in many countries. Sponsors of

British football, whether it was Canon sponsoring the Football League or Sharp sponsoring Manchester United, benefit from the spin-off that British football is seen on television all over the world.

One reason why some people have put money into sponsorship is that they were convinced – perhaps by a PR consultant – that it would achieve certain objectives better than advertising. The cost might have been the same, but probably less. In many cases, they have undoubtedly been proved right, and the process continues and expands. A quick scan through the sports section of The Sunday Times revealed the following examples of sponsorship, some by including the sponsor's name in the title of the event and some by clearly showing their name or logo on equipment or clothing.

- Cricket stumps showing the NatWest name and logo and Vodafone on the shoulders of the players
- Formula 1 drivers with Compaq emblazoned across their leathers
- The Smurfit Euro Open Golf Championship
- Credit Lyonnais very visible at the Tour de France
- Norwich Union written on every hurdle at an athletics meeting ...

But if you don't want to achieve any of those eleven objectives, forget it. Sponsorship is not for you.

What to sponsor?

If it is for you, the next stage is to decide what to sponsor. That's not easy. There is a whole world of wondrous things to sponsor, and plausible people who will take your money. There are people who want to break the record in walking backwards round the world. There are others who will pretend that a pile of bricks or Ms Emin's crumpled bed with dirty washing and a used condom on it is modern art. But there are also responsible organisations representing the sports, arts, education, expeditions and other endeavours which would not survive or succeed but for financial backing.

The choice will depend on your market. What kind of sponsorship is likely to reach large numbers of your potential customers most economically? We shall deal with costs later on. Does your product appeal to teenagers, the under-thirties, families, middle-aged mums – to whom? You need to be precise about this. Let's go through the various categories.

The five main categories are sports, arts and culture, publications, professional awards, and educational.

Sports

The range of sports that are interested in and, in some cases, only survive because of sponsorship, is limitless ...

Football	Rugby	Motor sport
Horse racing	Greyhound racing	Show jumping
Pony racing	Four-in-hand	Golf
Tennis	Badminton	Squash
Hockey	Curling	Netball
Basketball	Handball	Ice skating
Ice hockey	Skiing	Toboganning
Motorcycling	Veteran cars	Angling
Darts	Snooker	Bowls
Archery	Shooting	Yachting
Power boat racing	Flying	Hot air ballooning
Gliding	Hang gliding	Parachuting
Rowing	Canoeing	Surfing
Athletics	Cycling	Pigeon racing
Gymnastics	Boxing	Fencing
Wrestling	Road walking	Running
Marathons	Karting	Rock climbing
Mountaineering	Caving	Swimming
Diving	Water polo	Barge racing

... and for want of another category, competitive events like ballroom dancing, beauty contests, kite flying, traction-engine trials and ploughing matches!

Sponsorships can be of prizes, teams, individuals, equipment, or entire events such as games and tournaments. There can be multi-sponsorships, as with racing cars which bear the names of several sponsors. Or an event like a marathon can have a major sponsor of the event such as the Flora London Marathon, and many sub-sponsors of supplies. The choice is so wide, and the financial undertaking can be large or small, but there is almost certain to be something which will satisfy your objectives and reach your particular market.

Do not forget the village cricket or football team. One Gloucestershire fish and chip shop sponsors the village soccer team and, without doubt, they are the busiest chippie in the village, where there are two others within walking distance. Not only is the chippie seen to be interested and concerned about local sport, but is also recognised as being a major part of the community, because of their visible involvement at relatively low cost, in village life.

Arts and culture

Here again, you can choose from many options which include symphony orchestras, brass bands, music festivals, pop groups, performers, concerts, operas, ballets, theatres, records and CDs, art exhibitions, special exhibits at museums, literary prizes, drama festivals, archeological digs, historical places (e.g. National Trust), restorations, and wild life or environmental preservation or protection.

These are opportunities to reach particular publics, and to contribute to the cultural fabric of the country. Your company can be seen to be socially responsible, helping to maintain things that are precious to society, or encouraging talent. Famous theatres like Sadlers Wells, and costly symphony orchestras, would not survive but for sponsors – the visit in July 2000, for example, by the Kirov ballet was supported by The Daily Telegraph and their name appeared on posters, advertisements, programmes and so on, no doubt encouraging people to recognise their commitment to the arts and thus their worthiness as a newspaper.

Publications

Sponsored publications may be given away or sold and, like the world-famous Guinness publications, be a profitable business in itself. Cookery books, D-I-Y manuals, maps and guide books, and sports annuals may be sold through booksellers or by mail order. They provide a customer service, and may add prestige to a company's image.

Some sponsored books, with the imprint of a reputable publisher, are about technical subjects, written by in-house experts. Because of production costs, they require sponsorship from the company such as contribution to production costs and purchase of an agreed number of copies. Perhaps you have a wide knowledge of a subject which merits such an authoritative book?

Professional awards

Here is an inexpensive yet very effective form of sponsorship which may appeal to you. Awards may be given to journalists or photographers who cover your kind of product or industry. Or to specialist professionals like architects or civil engineers who may specify or use your products. Food manufacturers make awards to cookery writers, and camera manufacturers have annual awards for press photographers who use their cameras. Publicity can accrue from the function when the awards are presented, and the competition can encourage interest in your subject, and use of your products.

Educational

You may wish to encourage study of your subject or industry, and this can be done by sponsoring chairs, scholarships, academic books, bursaries and other educational awards. For example, Cable and Wireless sponsor students at City University, London, on a degree course leading to a BSc in Electrical and Electronic Engineering.

What about costs?

The third stage is what will it cost? Don't be misled into thinking that all you have to do is write a cheque or buy a nice trophy. There is a lot of organisational work to conduct. You may need to use some supportive advertising like arena boards at stadiums. There may be presentation ceremonies to organise, and various forms of hospitality may be desirable, necessary or possible.

You will need to make full use of PR opportunities and back-up such as media relations to ensure coverage, some system of evaluation, which may incur research services, and it may be a good idea to make a video for future PR use.

The sponsorship may be capable of all kinds of PR exploitation, and there may be many spin-off opportunities which should not be neglected. For example, some sponsorships lend themselves to case studies which can be published as articles, included in books or used in lectures, thus perpetuating them for some considerable time. Or in more hard cash terms, sponsorship may be exploited by your sales people who can provide free tickets to events, or host customers at events.

Very careful budgeting is essential. In the end, you still have to decide whether it is worth the money? But budgeting may also reveal unexpected benefits.

Finally, how will you organise it?

If you have a well-organised PR department, the whole thing can be planned and executed in-house. This may depend on the complexity of the sponsorship, and whether your people have not only the necessary know-how but, perhaps more important, the necessary time. Time is also another cost to consider.

There are many specialist PR consultancies which are skilled at both bringing together seekers of sponsorships and those who want to sponsor and organise the whole scheme. Their names and addresses will be found in Advertisers' Annual and the Hollis Press and Public Relations Annual (see bibliography), and the latter can also be visited at www.hollis-pr.co.uk.

Major firms are experienced in all the procedures and campaign planning and execution involved, and their initial advice is valuable if you are uncertain about the first three considerations outlined above.

Sponsorship is frequently featured in magazines such as

Marketing or PR Week and there is the specialist monthly Sponsorship News, with a web site at www.sponsorshipnews.com, which you will find particularly helpful in deciding whether or what to sponsor.

Sponsored broadcast programmes are fairly commonplace, with such programmes as plays and weather forecasts having acknowledged sponsors. Cultural events such as classical concerts are often co-sponsored by, say, British Gas or a national newspaper.

One last point – to be an acceptable sponsor, you need to have arrived. No-one wants to be sponsored by, or receive a prize or award from someone they've never heard of!

8

How Do I communicate with My Employees?

'Nobody tells me anything.'
John Galsworthy (James Forsyte in The Man of Property)

Ability to communicate with employees is not a particularly strong characteristic of the British business manager. Perhaps that is related to the curious class structure of the British, as exemplified by national press readership shown in Chapter 5. The old them and us, master and servant, Lords and Commons relationships persists. Managing directors don't dine in the canteen, Japanese fashion. Nor do we have worker directors, like the Germans. We still have rather quaint relics like the Conservative and Labour parties. Perhaps it's something to do with having royals.

Funnily enough, we pretend to be a democracy yet we deprive the majority of the electorate from being represented in Parliament and industrial democracy is virtually non-existent. Perhaps that's why some foreigners think the British hypocritical. But, of course, the home of democracy, Greece, was a slave state.

With this sort of castle and cottage background, management-employee relations tend to repeat that two-nation concept. Nevertheless, it has become a serious growth area of PR. Consultancies who conduct communication audits, have shown how little management knows about employee attitudes.

Have you ever tried to find out what your employees know about your organisation, and what they think of it? Has it ever occurred to you that they may know little about it, and think even less of it! This in spite of increased publicity about companies faced with mergers, takeovers, de-regulation and so on, and the greater openness in the media concerning businesses throughout the EU and the people who run them.

● How much do you tell your people about board room decisions and company policy?

● How much interest do you take in their attitudes and aspirations?

● To what extent do you exploit and encourage all the new technologies that make management-employee and employee-management communications much easier to practise? Like pagers, mobile phones, PCs?

● Do you know the difference between management-employee and employee-management communications, between downward and upwards and even sideways internal communications?

● Do you have anyone directly responsible for managing such communications? Now, there's a challenge! Maybe you think that is the responsibility of the personnel manager, or that a printed house journal is sufficient? But do you have either?

Maybe you are one of the enlightened minority of British business people who communicates well with your employees? Good for you. Britain is a great place for minorities.

A popular television series in 2000, 'Back to the Floor', showed what happened when top bosses actually went down to the shop floor and mucked in with the workforce. The mutual benefits were enormous and the quality of manager-worker and worker-manager communications was very high. The mutual understanding generated was unprecedented in most of the situations and the bemused bosses staggered back to their offices full of intent to generate even more cross-fertilisation of ideas and information. As an internal PR exercise, these visits and the resulting benefits were first class. It is to be hoped that the exercise was not just a one-off game carried out for the television series.

In spite of such ventures, we still live in a bemused world of industrial relations and staff relations, one the province of trade union negotiations and the other that of internal PR. It is an historic malfunction of management. When Ian McGregor left British Coal (remember them?) he made the point that there would never have been a strike if he had been allowed to talk to the miners instead of the union. Business today depends on a unified organisation (note that the word is not 'unionised'). Companies have been reduced to essential staff. Robotics in the factories and computers on the office desk have suddenly created a new structure of instant communication. It is now so easy to communicate, and there are far fewer people to communicate with.

We haven't reached the same advanced stage of worker directors and works councils like some businesses on the continent which have seldom if ever suffered a strike during the past forty years. We have only a few co-partnership firms, although they have been very successful. But we do have an increasing number of employee shareholders, and several hundred share option savings schemes have been operating through building societies since favoured by the 1980 Finance Act.

The days of the fuddy-duddy house journal, the crummy works outing and the benevolent Christmas beano have gone the way of paternal management. Now we can have instant mutual communication with an on-screen house journal. We have desk-top editing linked by satellite and on-line terminals world-wide, the news read as it is being written. We can also transmit messages rapidly by e-mail to individual employee mailboxes and zap information instantly on the internet and the intranet within larger organisations.

There is now no excuse for you to fail to communicate with your employees, or for them to fail to communicate with you. No matter where you all are!

Many UK companies have now taken on board such ideas as quality circles, which involve all the staff in seeking ideas to improve productivity. Groups, led by a supervisor, are organised at work station level, and they meet regularly. Their ideas go straight to management. In Singapore, under a different name, they are organised by the government with an annual contest between work improvement teams.

This is not to say that the traditional methods of internal communication are no longer valid, but good business communicators now use them more effectively. The house journal is the oldest form of organised or creative PR, but it is no longer a legitimate pulpit for paternal paymasters.

Internal communications are, like every other form of PR, a two-way process. Industrial unions in countries like Germany are happy to have works councils because it means having an inside knowledge of management plans. This is not so well received in Britain.

Politicians and unions apart, industry is becoming democratised by force of events, and wide-awake management has opportunities for adopting internal communication techniques. Neither discipline nor militancy works any more. Have you noticed this?

The first step is to find out what employees know, don't know, think and believe about the organisation.

What are their aspirations?

In any decade, aspirations change, but does management know what they now are? Are they security, higher pay, longer holidays, shorter working hours, greater safety, opportunities for promotion, equity ownership, more participation in decision making? Some of these aspirations have been discarded, but some are new.

Does management understand how employee aspirations have changed?

These anxieties and desires affect attitudes and opinions. The truth can be discovered by means of a communication audit whereby employees are surveyed with guaranteed confidentiality. This is very different from those old-fashioned and often misleading studies conducted by management consultants who had confidential chats with suspicious people and so often got it all wrong.

Communication audit

A communication audit, conducted by either an independent marketing research firm, or by a PR consultancy which offers this specialist service, can interview a representative sample of your employees with a guarantee of confidentiality.

A report can then be written which presents the opinions, awareness, misconceptions and so on (which cannot be attributed to individuals) so that management can appreciate what internal attitudes really are. This can be a revelation since normally management can only guess or assume, usually wrongly, what people think about their employer.

What assumptions do you make? Have you any idea how accurate they are?

One such survey, for instance, showed that while employees expected the company to make a profit, they believed the profits to be far in excess of what they actually were.

Another showed that employees were very critical of the company's advertising, and yet another showed that people thought they should have greater access to policy information. A great many strikes have resulted from rumour and inaccurate grapevine information. There are even companies where leaking information to the grapevine is thought to be an adequate means of informing employees!

It makes an interesting exercise to compare what you thought they thought, with the outcome of such a survey.

Another way of assessing employee opinions, or perhaps wishes, is to issue a questionnaire on a particular subject such as equity ownership, company cars, the house journal, staff uniforms, pension schemes, the new web site, the canteen, or other precise subjects, and to poll opinions. You will never know what people think unless you make the effort to find out. It is not often done. Management make all sorts of illogical assumptions. The answers could make all the difference to management-employee relations.

House journals

The printed house journal is still one of the most important forms of internal communication. Several hundred are published in Britain, and it is a popular medium throughout the world. In Third World countries, where newspapers and magazines may be few, house journals are to be found in many organisations. House journals have their own professional bodies such as the British Association of Communicators in Business (visit them at www.bacb.org.uk) and the International Association of Business Communicators, based in Brussels (www.iabc.com), both of which hold annual awards contests. In the USA, house journals have existed for more than a century.

If your organisation has a staff magazine or newspaper, how do you regard it? As a means of communicating with employees? As a means by which they can communicate with you? Or as a means by which they can communicate with each other? These three purposes concern downward, upward and sideways communication. All three are important.

The modern trend is to satisfy all three communication processes. They are best encouraged if the editor is independent, and not muzzled by managerial restraints. Editorial committees are justified only if they help the editor, but not if they are used to police the work. Committees are seldom creative.

Unless a house journal is valued by readers, it is a waste of money. Be bold and ask these questions.

? Do the staff welcome each issue?

? Do they regard it rather cynically as something imposed on them by management?

? Are employees invited to contribute to the contents? Reader participation is important.

? Are readers' critical letters permitted?

? Is reader interest stimulated by the inclusion of sales and wants classified ads?

? Does it look like the sort of magazine or newspaper they would normally buy, or does it merely satisfy the vanity of management?

Too many house journals are unrealistic, too prestigious and so often printed on heavyweight or shiny surface paper quite unlike a normal commercial publication. If it is a tabloid newspaper it should look like one, printed on newsprint and not look like a glossy sales leaflet. If you have one of these glossy heavyweights, whose fault is it? Did you insist on the sort of journal you wanted? One well-known editor insists that his fortnightly newspaper should look like and be as good as the popular daily that most of the factory workers buy. This extends to hiring well-known Fleet Street feature writers who are known to his readers.

Do you appreciate this sort of psychology? Do you make sure that the budget is well spent in producing a journal that is effective in achieving good management-employee relations?

With desk-top publishing using PCs or Macs, it is possible to edit and design magazines quickly and efficiently. But if the creative skills are not possessed in-house, there are several excellent consultancies which specialise in house journal production. There are also printers who specialise in printing house journals and have design studio services.

E-newspapers

Internal information can also be made available on a web site, with or without hard copy, whereby pages or items can be viewed wherever the reader happens to have a PC and modem. This can be done equally easily on an internal net, so that everyone in the works can have simple and easy access to information. Web site material can, of course, be read by anyone at all who has access to the web, so promulgating your company's image and news to every little corner of the world.

Video magazines

The newsreel type of house journal, which can be played back on a VCR at the workplace or in the home, has become popular. Material can also be read from a CD-ROM and some hi-tec-aware companies are using this medium to send out company information. A few larger companies have their own video studio for the production of training, documentary and video house journal programmes. The visual effect of this medium is more intimate than the printed word. It can help employees to know management and other people in the organisation and vice versa. It has the authority, authenticity, familiarity and realism of television with its combination of sound, movement and colour.

Videos are also useful for explaining the annual report and accounts to employees, and some companies make sure that all their employees see such videos as quickly as possible after the AGM and publication of the accounts. A typical device is to have the managing director interviewed by a TV personality, and for graphic presentations to be made by means of animation or computer graphics. The same video can be distributed to shareholders, and shown at the AGM.

Notice boards

Have you looked at your notice boards lately? What are they like? Organised and controlled notice boards can be an effective way of achieving internal communications, especially between employees themselves as when there are staff societies and activities. The items can be produced and positioned by a central editing office such as the PR department. When people know where to find what they want to know about, this kind of notice-board is a simple form of communication. It encourages communication.

The above are some examples, but there are many more devices which may be particularly appropriate to certain organisations. There are wall newspapers, audio-tapes, wall posters, letters to employees, open-door policies, 'speak-up' and suggestion box schemes, staff meetings, quality circles and so on. Today, the techniques are so many and so varied that there is no excuse for poor management-employee relations, except bad management.

9

Do I Need an In-house PR Department?

'There is only one thing in the world worse than being talked about, and that is not being talked about.'
Oscar Wilde, The Picture of Dorian Gray

Who handles public relations within your organisation? Is it part of your job, whether you are in top management or a department manager in charge of, say, personnel, sales, marketing or advertising? Perhaps no-one in particular is responsible for public relations! You may never have even thought about it. Or you may rely solely on the services of your advertising agency or public relations consultancy.

Of course, if you are a small business with only a few (or even just one) employees, the PR function must fall on someone who already probably wears several hats. The necessity to set up and enjoy good public relations is for every business. Maybe not on a global scale for Fred Fernackerpans who runs a one-man window-cleaning business, but he cannot afford to alienate the local community and must do what he can on his own to make himself and his business appear desirable, wholesome and efficient as well as an integral part of local life.

A lot depends on how you see public relations. Maybe you think it is sufficient to let your advertising agency indulge in product publicity, or engage a PR consultancy to send out news releases and organise PR functions? Perhaps you use a consultancy only for specialist corporate and financial matters?

And yet, PR concerns the total communications of your total organisation.

Hardly something to handle in a casual or slipshod fashion, is it? Or to bury in some other department like marketing.

Unlike advertising, which may be best placed with an agency where you can share the skills of a planning, creative and media buying team, PR calls for an intimate knowledge of the inner workings of your organisation at all levels. Public relations requires the integration of knowledge and communicators.

That is why the majority of advertising personnel work in agencies, while the reverse is true of PR personnel. This is also because there are hundreds of organisations, particularly those that are non-commercial or are in the public sector, which do no advertising (except maybe recruitment) but are engaged in organised PR.

Unless the PRO knows what's going on, how can he or she act as your spokesperson? A first consideration, then, is the positioning of the PRO. Public relations is not a part-time job for someone like the Marketing Services Manager. It is a full-time role, and ideally the in-house PRO (whatever the job title and, like Heinz, there are more than 57 varieties) should be directly answerable to the chief executive. In fact, in most large organisations, he or she is a board director, and designated Director of Public Relations or Public Affairs Director. So, at this early juncture, let's see the PR department as an independent one, servicing all other functions of your business such as works, personnel, marketing and financial management. The PRO should be part of the top management team and should know more about the organisation than anybody else in it. The PRO needs to share everybody's confidences.

Does this surprise you? Had you thought of the in-house PRO being no more than a press officer, a dogsbody, and maybe someone attached to another department?

Well, it all depends on how seriously you not only need to but want to communicate. It comes down to objectives. What are your PR objectives? When these have been defined, you will probably find that to achieve them a properly managed, staffed, equipped and funded independent department is necessary.

Public relations is not just about favourable mentions, images and climates of opinion. Tell that to British Telecom, favourite Aunt Sally of the British press! Let us consider some typical PR objectives, and see whether they justify having an in-house PR department.

Typical PR objectives

1. To *improve local communications* and to make the company's business better known and understood locally, especially by the local authority, public services, colleges and the general public.

   Community relations will require regular liaison with local media, involvement in local events, and the organisation of various open days and group visits.

2. To *maintain employee stability*. Money has been invested in recruitment and training, and the company depends on skills.

   Improved management-employee relations will call for some of the activities and media discussed in Chapter 7. A more participatory, printed house journal, or the development of video or e-communications, are necessary for starters.

3. To *educate the market* about improved products due to the introduction of new techniques.

   A consumer and trade press campaign of news releases, feature articles, press receptions and photography will be necessary for the market education programme.

4. To *raise money* for new developments, for which a new share issue is to be floated.

   The share issue will require liaison with the bankers underwriting the flotation, with the Stock Exchange and with the financial PR consultants engaged.

5. To *support the company's presence* at UK exhibitions and overseas trade fairs.

If the company is to participate in home and overseas exhibitions, there will need to be liaison over several months with the press officers of the UK exhibitions, and at least with the Department of Trade, British Trade International (formerly the British Overseas Trade Board) and the Central Office of Information regarding overseas shows.

We have confined ourselves to five very different PR objectives which are likely to be enough to occupy an in-house PRO for a year, and even then he or she would probably need at least the ad hoc services of a financial PR consultant for the share issue. Now let us go back over these five commitments and consider with whom the PRO will need to liaise in order to achieve these five objectives.

- The community relations programme will require liaison with the chief executive, personnel manager and works manager.
- The internal programme will involve the same people.
- Handling PR for new products will mean liaison with the marketing, advertising and production people especially.
- The share issue will call for liaison with the chief executive, company secretary and financial director.
- Exhibitions will involve the PRO with marketing, advertising and export managers.

From this, it will be seen that the in-house PRO has to work with all the management functions within the business. She has to share confidences with everyone, and often this calls for advance knowledge of what is proposed or agreed, and not be told or find out when it is too late. Often, she needs to be involved in the decision making process because of the public relations implications of many decisions.

The in-house PRO should be the eyes, ears and voice of the organisation. She should have access to any information at all times. She should know as much as, if not more than, the chief executive. It is not a game for the boss's beautiful wife, as in Dynasty, nor a crusade by a hatchet man for a President or Prime Minister as we have seen in the USA and the UK. Remember the myth we demolished way back – PR is **not** about white-washing or creating an impression that is unreal, or doctoring the spin to suit the boss.

Yes, an in-house PR department and manager is necessary in any substantial business. It should be divorced from any second-cousin activity like marketing or advertising. It should be answerable to top management, and should service all other departments.

This is not to say that the in-house PR department is superior to the PR consultant, or that the PR consultant is inferior to the in-house PR department. They are different and they may complement each other. The situation is quite different from that which applies in advertising. Most advertising people work in advertising agencies. This is because an advertiser shares the skills of an agency team over short periods. But PR goes on all the time and touches on the activities of the entire organisation. Because of this intimate, internal aspect of PR (even when dealing with external affairs), the in-house PRO is essential. Perhaps this, if nothing else, will emphasise the great difference between advertising and public relations.

Moreover, an outside PR consultancy is more likely to work successfully with the client if there is an in-house PRO who understands what the consultancy is trying to do. The two can then merge their special strengths and compensate for their weaknesses. For example, the in-house PRO will not deal with such a wide range of media and techniques as the consultant, while the consultant will have nothing like the in-house PRO's knowledge of his company or industry.

Who should do it?

Who and what sort of person should head up the in-house PR function? Should it be a man or a woman? How do you find such a person?

The choice of a man or a woman may depend on what business you are in. Women are very successful in PR, often because they worry about details and are good organisers. Again, it depends on age, experience, qualifications, salary and personal qualities.

The professional qualifications are the CAM Diploma which requires three years study and is near-degree standard, while a full Member of the Institute of Public Relations is elected on the basis of a minimum of five years' comprehensive experience and the recommendation of two sponsors.

While young people such as graduates or those with business studies qualifications do enter PR, many recruits make PR a second or third career, bringing with them experience which is valuable to the job. It may be experience of an industry such as yours.

Most important are the personal qualities required by PR work. He or she needs to be a good communicator, and this embraces all forms of communication such as writing, speaking, computing, photography and – frequently nowadays – the use of video.

Ability to plan and organise, budget and manage a department is also important. So, too, is ability to work with all kinds of people, and to have personal integrity so that he or she is trusted both inside and outside the organisation. In addition, imagination is necessary because PR includes a great deal of creative work. Ability to use a PC is essential.

It is not a job for your favourite nephew just because he is your favourite nephew! Nor is it a form of sideways promotion for someone you want to move out of an existing job.

To find such a person, you may need to employ a head hunter, but vacancies are advertised mainly in PR Week, Campaign and the Monday edition of The Guardian.

10

Do I Need a PR consultancy?

'Remember that time is money.'
Benjamim Franklin

This is not quite the same question as 'Do I need an in-house PR department?' Nor is it the same as 'Do I need an advertising agency?' The point at which you would normally appoint a PR consultancy could be the opposite to that when you appointed an advertising agency, and you could use a PR consultancy as well as have your own PR department.

This probably sounds confusing, and it may not be helped by the fact that in recent years advertising agencies have been jumping on the PR bandwagon.

Advertising agencies probably know as much about PR as PR consultancies know about advertising. It's rather like inviting Ian Paisley to preach at St. Peter's in Rome. The reason for this is that it is usual to appoint an advertising agency when it is no longer good enough to do your own advertising. You need creative talent and media planning and buying skills, and the advertising budget now justifies both seeking an agency and being an economic proposition to one. But with PR, a consultancy may be employed until the volume of work (and fee) warrants setting up an in-house PR department.

It does not stop there. Even when a PR department exists, a PR consultancy may be employed for two reasons. The first is to augment a busy PR department, and to gain an outside view from time to time. The second is to provide specialised services, maybe on an ad hoc basis, which the PR department is less able to provide itself.

From these remarks, it should be obvious that PR consultancies – and they are not agencies because they do earn commission – can offer special services and advantages.

There are some 1,200 consultancies listed in the Hollis Press and Public Relations Annual and they come and go by the week. You need to be careful about choosing one. The larger ones belong to the Public Relations Consultants Association. But anyone can call himself or herself a consultant, and credentials and proof of performance need to be checked out. For instance, even if the consultancy is not a member of the PRCA, its individual management ought to be members of the Institute of Public Relations. (Check out www.prca.org.uk for information on the Association and their aims and interests, and www.ipr.org.uk for details of the Institute.)

But there are a lot of cowboys and cowgirls, especially the latter. Having been warned, you should also be aware of the strengths and weaknesses of consultancies, and of the special services they can offer.

What are their strengths? Mainly, it is the breadth of experience gained in handling many accounts for a variety of clients over a number of years. It is not difficult to check out such mature qualities. A good firm should be proud of its record and have case studies to show you. But unlike advertising agencies, PR firms can be quite small and still perfectly proficient. Advertising calls for a great deal of expensive specialised work whereas in PR, the practitioner tends to be more of a jack-of-all-trades. Don't be misled by the fact that in advertising, different people do separate jobs but in PR one person does the lot. The result is that, of necessity, the PR person is more versatile.

Some of this range of skills and experience comes from training, some from experience. One way of judging the ability of a PR consultant to give you the service you want is to test what he knows. There is no place in PR for the smooth operator or pretty girl as so often depicted in fiction. (Mind you, this does not mean that they *have* to be rough and ugly!) The successful PR consultant has to be able to give sound professional advice, and to carry out programmes with skill and efficiency. Moreover, fees are seldom high (compared with expenditure on advertising) and he has to work within budgets to satisfy clients and to make a profit. He has to be a good business manager in both your interests and his own.

The PR consultancy world is less flamboyant and ivory-towered than advertising. Perhaps this is because the PR consultant is such a jack-of-all-trades and more down-to-earth.

Does this surprise you? Did you think PR consultancies were glamour rather than work shops? Did you think it was a world of El Vino Fleet Street contacts, lavish press receptions, and lunching lady journalists at posh restaurants? Some prospective clients do think that PR is all about socialising, but the gin and tonic image died twenty years ago. This is not to say that a skilled PR practitioner should not be civilised enough to read a wine list as well as an airline timetable. Nowadays, a main difference between advertising agencies and PR consultancies is how the money is spent and how you, the client, have to pay.

The big items in an advertising budget are the media purchases and production costs. In PR, time is the major cost factor, and this is charged out on a daily or hourly rate. In fact, the only thing the PR practitioner has to sell is the value of his expertise and experience as an hourly rate. To make a profit, he has to recover all his costs (e.g. his time and that of his staff, and his overheads and running costs) plus a percentage for profit, and calculate this on a daily or hourly basis. So, when you enter into a contract with a consultancy, you agree to a programme which represents a certain volume of time as represented by an annual fee.

Each client buys so much time, and the consultancy employs staff accordingly, and they keep time sheets and record how the time allocated to each client is spent. If the consultancy is to stay in business and make a profit, it has to budget and use time properly, otherwise it will go bust. It is dishonest to rob a big client to subsidise a small one, and it is suicidal to charge a small or new client a low fee in order to get an account in the hope that it will grow and eventually pay a bigger fee.

You have to understand how the finances of consultancies differ from those of advertising agencies. A professional service is no different from anything else you buy: on the whole you get what you pay for.

There are two reasons why clients may be dissatisfied with PR consultancies: they either pay too small a fee to justify a worthwhile service, or they demand more than they are paying for.

You cannot expect a four-bedroom house if you are paying for only a bungalow. The best way to get your money's worth is to know what you want in the first place. Do you want a bungalow or a four bedroom house?

A lot of clients don't actually know what they want. They know they want some advertisements in the press or on TV in order to sell their goods – to the trade as well as to the consumer. Do you know what you want from a consultancy, or do you just want to be in fashion and have a consultancy just like some people have a tank of tropical fish in the reception lounge?

Have you discovered from reading this book this far that you need either an in-house PR department or a PR consultancy or both? Do you know why?

Costing a consultancy service

A PR programme will take time to discuss, plan and carry out. To this must be added the costs of materials such as photography, print and other physical items, plus expenses such as travelling expenses and hospitality. Unless there are very heavy printing, video or exhibition costs, the biggest cost is likely to be time.

Don't forget that time includes regular meetings to discuss progress and maybe changes of plan. It costs money to talk to a PR consultant, just as it does to talk to a doctor, architect, lawyer or engineer. That is normal professional practice. You may have been spoiled by an advertising agent who lavishes time on you – but only because the media are paying for it and virtually subsidising you.

To demonstrate this, we will consider a brief idea of a consultancy budget, the sort of thing you could expect to find in a proposition from a consultant. Real figures are not used because the hourly rate will depend on whether the consultancy is in London or the regions and according to the quality of the service. A few consultancies also vary the hourly rate according to the seniority of the account executive who will handle your account.

The style of the budget may differ but the following is set out to show you how a fee is calculated. The consultant may start with a given budget which represents a certain number of hours or workload, or he may calculate what it will cost to carry out a specific programme. This is like asking what kind of house you can build for so much money, or 'what would it cost to build a four bedroom house with a double garage?'

To explain this more clearly, if a hypothetical £50 per hour is taken as a consultant's hourly rate, the first line of the budget means that if there are regular monthly meetings between you and the consultant, averaging three hours, this item would cost twelve times three (hours) times £50 per hour, totalling £1800. The number of hours will depend on whether the consultant has to travel to the meeting. If the consultant is in London and you are in the North of England, travel time has also to be included at the hourly rate.

Seven hours are allowed for a press reception. On the day, it may occupy a couple of hours, but over the preceding two or three months time will have been spent in odd spells such as writing the wording of invitations, talking to the banqueting manager at the venue, writing speeches, taking photographs, writing releases, reading proofs, sending out invitations and numerous organisational details. Another budget will also be necessary for the material costs and expenses in addition to time (which is represented by fee).

This is a good point to reiterate that the fee covers time and only time, for obvious reasons. Normally, a consultancy makes no profit on purchased materials or on expenses such as catering at a press reception.

You may come across the expression 'retainer' or even use it yourself. In the PR world, the term is a misnomer and it is often used wrongly and misleadingly. A retainer is not a fee. As with a lawyer's retainer, a retainer means what it says. It retains the services of a professional consultant, usually exclusive of competitors. That is all. When services are performed, they are paid for on the basis of manhours,

Job	Frequency	Hours per job	Hourly rate	Total cost
Monthly progress meeting	12	3	£xx	£xxxx
Press receptions	3	7	£xx	£xxxx
Exhibition support	3	7	£xx	£xxxx
News releases	12	3	£xx	£xxxx
Feature article	3	7	£xx	£xxxx
Organising facility visits	3	21	£xx	£xxxx
Preparing annual reports	1	14	£xx	£xxxx
and so on, plus estimated costs of materials and expenses				

materials and expenses. No work can be expected for a retainer, only the right to the consultant's services exclusively. Chapter 20 deals with this specifically, but a sensible approach to engagement of a consultancy is to invite it to carry out research to see what communication problems exist and need to be solved by a planned PR programme. You would normally do this before putting money into an advertising campaign, so why not in the case of PR? This cost – it's really an insurance – has to be added to the fee. Research is comparatively new in PR but things are changing. Fewer clients just blunder into PR programmes. They investigate the situation, know what they want, and set out to achieve definite objectives.

So beware of the PR consultancy which is prepared to take your money on the basis of vague instructions or promises. Within six months, you will be demanding to know what you are getting for your money. Your demand should really be satisfied before signing a contract of service.

Special consultancy services

One of the chief reasons for engaging a PR consultancy, and one that is attractive even if you have your own in-house PR department, is that there are many specialist firms which offer certain services.

It would be uneconomic to run these services internally on a full-time basis, and they may be ones that are required only occasionally. Moreover, they are ones where very special expertise is involved such as designing, finance or politics. Let us consider some of them and see whether or not they apply to your business.

Some consultancies tend to specialise in particular interests or industries such as fashion, entertainment, motor-cars or hi-technology. But others are even more specialised and four principal groups are:

Corporate and financial

Mostly based in the City of London, these consultancies deal with all-the-year-round corporate PR or public affairs, and particularly with financial matters. The latter include interim and annual reports, AGMs, share issues, flotations, mergers and take-over bids. These activities are controlled by Stock Exchange rules, legislation and other formalities, calling for expert knowledge.

In recent years, mergers, deregulation and take-over bids have seen the expansion of several PR consultancies specialising in financial PR. Privatisation, with its new additional objectives of popularising share ownership, required educational PR literature to explain share ownership to new investors. Takeover bids have been so aggressive and financially vast that they have seen 'knocking' campaigns which have provoked criticism, as has the recent proliferation of mutual societies converting to banks. There have also been insider scandals, and a new vigilance towards representatives of target and predator companies (such as PR consultancies).

Since the Big Bang in October 1986, the London Stock Exchange has changed enormously, especially with the extensive use of computerised systems such as SEAQ, the Stock Exchange Automated Quotations service and SETS, the Stock Exchange Order Book system, in operation since October 1997. The Stock Exchange also produces relevant publications with daily, weekly and less frequent analyses and details which are readily available. Although these systems make is clearer and easier to grasp what is going on, you would be wise to use a financial PR consultancy rather than get it wrong with the authorities. You may not be in the take-over business, but shareholder relations – especially with the institutions – can still be important. You may not want to be a target victim, or you may be an expansive predator. Expert advice and well organised activities will be necessary either way.

Parliamentary liaison and lobbying

This concerns not only the Houses of Parliament and the civil service but the EU and the European Parliament. The PR consultancy service takes two main forms: advising clients of Parliamentary proceedings which matter to them, e.g. impending legislation, White Papers, Green Papers, readings of Bills, receiving of evidence by committees and royal commissions; and lobbying (or presenting information) to relevant MPs and ministers.

Strict Houses of Parliament rules have to be obeyed, and Members of Parliament have to record their outside interests. The IPR and the PRCA maintain registers of their members who are Members of either House of Parliament.

Parliamentary PR does not mean PR between Parliament and the outside world, or on behalf of Parliament itself. Nor does it mean the bribing of MPs to give favourable support to a client. 'Cash for questions' is now a phrase ingrained in popular folklore about the way some MPs have been financially inveigled into asking pertinent questions in Parliament on behalf of their paymasters.

A number of MPs receive substantial fees for advising outside organisations. This has been criticised. But their advice could be vital to a company which might be penalised by new legislation if its views were not presented at the right time to the right people. Democracy does take heed of the views of interested parties, and pressure groups are expressions of democracy. You may find this kind of PR vital to your business.

Corporate identity

We have already discussed corporate identity schemes in Chapter 3. There are famous creative consultancies who produce original schemes incorporating logo, house colour, typography, livery and their applications.

House journal editing

Several firms edit and produce house journals for clients, and while most house journals are produced in-house, you may not have your own editor and a specialist consultancy could be a practical answer. They will supply professional writing and design, and work with printers familiar with this type of work.

From these examples you will see that the consultancy world is versatile and competent, and has moved a long way from the press relations services of the past. A number are broad-based, embracing marketing communications and applying themselves to marketing problems. Many, today, are proud to give prospective clients printed case studies, slide or video presentations which demonstrate their work for clients.

We began by comparing the appointment of an advertising agency and a PR consultancy. You may think it is expensive to hire a consultancy, and that the hourly rate is exorbitant. You could be surprisingly wrong. The cost of a consultancy service has to be judged by what you get for your money. Remember, PR is not a luxury. You do not have to spend money on PR, but you might be very foolish not to. It is rather like insurance. A policy costs money, and you might think it expensive – but not when you have a fire, accident or burglary.

Unless you have clear-cut PR objectives, there is no point in spending money on PR.

But the effectiveness of PR can be remarkable. It can even be more measurable than advertising, and certainly less costly – if you have objectives which can be seen to have been achieved or not. We shall return to this in Chapter 22. You may be too impatient to wait until you reach the end of this book, so why not read the chapter on evaluation now?

Coming back to that seemingly high hourly rate, a consultancy does not earn that for every working hour of its available time. It does have to look after its own business affairs such as recruiting staff, training staff, getting new clients, doing its accounts, sending out bills and other routine matters which can take up a great deal of its time. This is one reason why very small consultancies go out of business.

If you do not have your own PR department, and decide to use a consultant, at which point does it become viable to set up your own in-house PR department?

It may cost more than you think. Don't make the mistake of thinking that because the annual fee has reached a certain figure, it might be cheaper to run your own PR unit. It might be better, but not necessarily cheaper. Suppose you were employing a consultancy five days a week, that is, virtually full-time. If the rate was £100 per hour the fee would be £180,000 a year. That would be a very busy account for a large company.

But what could you get for £180,000 if you spent it in-house? You would need, at least, an equally skilled, experienced and qualified PRO and a first-class secretary; offices (including rent and rates), all the necessary computers and other equipment (including depreciation) and servicing with light, heat, telephone, cleaning, the cost of insurances, holidays (the consultancy operates all-the-year round), and you would probably need an assistant to provide back-up. The PRO would also need a car. You would still have to pay the same price for materials and expenses such as printing, stationery, postage, copying, catering, hospitality and travel. And if you did have your own in-house PR department you would probably find more uses for it, and this would cost even more on staff and equipment.

So, as already said, although it might be better to have your own PR department it is unlikely to be cheaper. Very likely, you would then find other, more specialised uses for a PR consultancy.

11

Is Corporate Advertising Necessary?

'The verdict of the world is conclusive.'
St Augustine, Contra Epist.Parmen., iii.24

There was a time when corporate, prestige or institutional advertising was the advertising world's concept of public relations. Judging by some of the ads, mostly in full colour, which appear in business newspapers and magazines like Fortune and The Economist, it still is! Television viewers, used to hard-selling ads for detergents and dog foods, have been perplexed by corporate commercials because they did not seem to be selling anything.

It is difficult to tell what some corporate ads are supposed to do beyond fill the coffers of publishers and advertising agents. They make a lot of journals look very pretty.

True, it has been said that a company needs to be seen. There are cheaper and probably more effective ways of doing it than full-colour press advertising, although it seems to appeal to Arab banks.

The improbability of the value of corporate advertising is evident when you think deeply about your favourite business magazine, for example, and try to remember some of the pages of full-colour corporate ads, and recall the names of some of the advertisers. You will probably be oblivious to what they were saying and to fail to remember their strapline slogans. This is frequently because the advertisers choose inappropriate journals for their glossy ads, such as chemical companies advertising in The Economist or banks advertising in Chlorine Week.

However, an Economist reader who receives a postal questionnaire about the latest Audi is an example of better targeting.

If corporate advertising is to be justified – and the scepticism expressed above is not meant to imply that it cannot work – you have to ask two questions. What do I want it to achieve and to whom should it be addressed?

One wonders how often these questions are ever asked. So many corporate advertising campaigns seem to have a standard media schedule, of which The Economist is an example. The Economist is probably the last place to put some of the corporate advertising which contributes to its weekly bulk. There are times when it would be appropriate to put corporate ads in popular newspapers like the Sun and the Mirror. Tate and Lyle have done so.

What is the purpose of corporate advertising, and why must advertising be used for PR purposes? Some good questions there!

To take the second question first, the only justification for using advertising for PR purposes is when it is essential to state exactly what you want to say, to do it as boldly as possible, and to do it in certain media on a certain date. In other words, you want to have complete control of your message. There have been some good examples of this from Virgin Trains and from Orange, for example.

The answer to the first question is that corporate advertising aims to enhance the corporate image by saying favourable things about it. In a sense, that is a perverse form of PR for surely advertising is what you say about yourself and PR is what others say about you?

But, of course, the media tend to assume that bad news is good news and good news is no sort of news at all.

Corporate advertising can therefore serve the purpose of presenting the good news about an organisation which the media would not normally print. This is a tendentious argument because it admits the failure of traditional media relations.

Given that such a situation exists, corporate advertising can be a legitimate form of PR, adopting a positive tactic in urgent circumstances. This is very different from merely flying the flag which is what so much of this sort of advertising seems to be. Serious corporate advertising therefore has a purpose: it aims to convey an urgent message to a selected public.

Let us take a hypothetical example. Suppose your company has suffered bad publicity because of a series of set-backs. Your share price has fallen. The trade is wary. All sorts of risks exist. You could lose orders, key staff could desert you, and a takeover bid might well be imminent. And yet you know that the truth is very different. There is no need for panic. You have a new factory coming on-stream to produce a market-leader, and the good news is about to break. To stop the rot, and create a favourable market situation, you could place a confidence-booster corporate advertising campaign in journals as varied as the Financial Times, the trade, technical, professional and local press, plus the leading nationals read by your distributors and customers.

Now that would be a real purpose-built corporate campaign which was aimed at the right people in order to actually do something. In fact, this sort of campaign was adopted by an American multi-national and it ran for three years. The ads used pithy copy which hammered home facts to destroy misconceptions which had been carefully researched. They did not use pretty coloured pictures; instead they used dramatic headlines and typography.

There is another kind of corporate advertising which is very effective and that is issue or advocacy advertising. Used by Mobil in the States, it has been dubbed Op-ed advertising because such advertisements have been deliberately placed opposite leader-page editorials. The objectives of this kind of PR advertising are two-fold as will be explained. In a sense, this is a kind of lobbying or pressuring via the media – usually the press, but TV can be used.

Whereas the typical British corporate advertising is full of pretty pictures and highly literary copy, and talks of great achievements, historical record or the excellence of its research, the American-style issue advertising tackles issues of the day. Either it positions the corporation in relation to government policies on, say, pollution, the environment, nuclear power, drugs or crime, or it presents the case for an industry under attack from either government or pressure groups.

Oil companies have used media such as the Sunday colour magazines and TV to show how they are protecting wild life or are engaged in other energy industries. Leading up to privatisation, a number of enterprises have used corporate advertising to establish a corporate image. We have also seen companies using this form of PR to explain their diversification when they were often thought to merely monopolise in one industry. Issue advertising is not quite like the propaganda ads which certain interested parties published in Britain in the 1960s and '70s to protect themselves from the Labour governments' nationalisation plans.

Issue advertising seeks to create better understanding of a company's attitude, position or even desire to support some typical and maybe controversial subject. Here we have a very positive use of advertising for a PR purpose.

It is vital to distinguish between vanity and purposeful institutional advertising.

There are, of course, other kinds of corporate and financial advertising which are legitimate. You may wish to present your company's case during an industrial dispute, or publish a summary of the annual report, and the offer of a copy of the full report may be advertised. This is an exercise that can readily be conducted on the internet, also giving an opportunity to interested people to respond to your information. This in turn will help you to gauge the public's reactions to your stance.

Decide why you need corporate advertising.

- Is it to present a case quickly in words and media of your choosing?

- Is it to position yourself firmly in the market place?

- Is it to clearly identify and establish your corporate image (which is called image advertising)?

- Do you want to put on record your achievements, which a number of Japanese companies have done in international media?

- Do you wish to inform other corporate and individual technophiles that you are as thoroughly up-to-date with your technology (if not better than that) as anyone else?

- Do you want to show how you are responding to government policies, or contributing to social issues as Shell and BP have done?

- Maybe you want to show the contribution you are making to the economy, as ITT have done, or to demonstrate the quality of your staff and career opportunities as IBM have done?

- Perhaps you think it necessary to be competitive, as aircraft manufacturers have done.

These are all very positive aims. Prestige derives from such advertising, but that is not its sole purpose.

12

How Do I Conduct
Good Customer Relations

'For evil news rides post, while good news baits.'
John Milton

How much of your business comes from recommendations?

Some companies seem to be naturally family favourites. Our biggest advertiser, Cadbury Schweppes, would not be so successful if people had not liked their products for generations. But why do people stick to the same brands? It's not just because of the advertising or habit buying. Consumers can be very fickle, easily diverted by a sales promotion give-away. Good customer relations are the roots of public relations. How are yours – or do you wish they were better?

Good customer relations are the essence of the success of Marks and Spencer, although this has been under some stress. People from all quarters of the world visit their stores. It was the basis of Jesse Boot's success when he laid out his medicines on an open counter where people could see them. It was Gordon Selfridge who made shopping fun. There is nothing new about developing good customer relations.

Why is it that for many years people buy the same make of motor-car? Because, being fed up with some marques that seem to be in love with their service engineers, people stick with a marque whose owners, without exception, praise it. That is good enough recommendation for most folk.

How do you make people like you, and not just you personally but your business, your products or services?

The Japanese have scored all over the world – and largely at the expense of the British – by simply making things that work. If you ever visit Hong Kong or Singapore, have a game counting British cars. You won't need many fingers.

However, the customer satisfaction that accrues from a good product or service is only the beginning of good customer relations. Customer satisfaction certainly creates good reputation and encourages recommendation. But it has to be nurtured, maintained and sustained, and that is where PR techniques come in. It calls for PR-minded management in both boardroom and departments down the line.

Let us consider the reverse of this for the moment. Great customer satisfaction may result from the many clever technological devices, and the use of new materials such as plastics, which we all enjoy. Until they go wrong! For example, the life expectancy of many electronic products is alarmingly brief in spite of their cost. When spares or repairs are required, they are either expensive or the model has been replaced by the next generation of wizardry, and one is expected to buy a new one. This applies to most office equipment such as computers, word processors and copiers, and to domestic items such as cookers, hi-fi equipment, dish-washers, videos and lawn mowers. A common complaint from customers is 'Nothing lasts these days!' Talk about built-in obsolescence – it's worse today than when the Americans invented it in the 1930s.

Modern production, replacing metal with flimsy plastics, concerned with economies not only of manufacturer but of inventory control of stocks of spares, is often cynical regarding customer relations. Costings are based too narrowly on short-term profit, not on long-term customer relations. Profits are related to wear-out factors, not durability. The textile industry, for instance, discovered that man-made fibres lasted too long, and re-introduced cotton and wool!

Are your customers victims of such policies? It can have its penalties in export markets where spares and servicing can be critical reasons for buying, and durability is a major selling point. Africa is littered with broken down Western technology from power stations to transistor radios.

One of the reasons why the Japanese have resisted imports is that their quality is so poor by Japanese standards.

What is the secret of good customer relations?

It's not only using clever PR techniques, although we shall come to them, but something which is inherent in the nature of the PR. It is about how your company is seen to behave and about goodwill and reputation. If PR is about creating understanding, building goodwill and respect, and changing attitudes, it depends on two-way communications. You have to listen as well as talk. This may mean welcoming complaints and having a system of dealing with them.

Good customer relations spring from being aware of, or finding out, what customers want or would like. What problems does the product or the service have to solve in order to produce customer satisfaction? What expectations does it provoke? What doubts does it invite?

These considerations can apply to the most elementary product. Take a clothes peg, for example. Does it hold the washing firmly on the line, is it easily lost, does it go rusty, does it snap? What are the customers' experiences and reactions? Do you know, or do you go on making the same product, assuming it pleases everyone?

Do you think these are silly questions? They are certainly not asked by motor-car manufacturers who ship out cars to the tropics without changing the cold-weather equipment necessary in the northern hemisphere. Yet manufacturers of combine harvesters produce different machines for different crops, seasons, conditions and terrains.

One of the cleverest examples of good customer relations was the packing of Aspro – about seventy years ago! – in paper strips which could be kept in the pocket or handbag. Usually, aspirins were packed in clumsy glass bottles.

Putting plastic handles on heavy cans of paint and snap-open pourers on juice cartons; putting medicinal tablets in blister packs; creating disposable handkerchiefs, nappies, razors and lighters; supplying handy aerosols; and use of correct quantity sachets or individual packs for so many products which need to be measured, all help to sell these products. Why? Because they serve the convenience of the customer, whether they may be cheaper to produce or actually cost the customer more.

A corollory of this is that much of present-day packaging seems to have a high irritation factor – milk cartons that cannot be opened without fountains of milk everywhere, child-proof caps that baffle even dextrous adults, shrink-wrapping that is so tight you break your fingernails trying to prise it off. These things do not encourage a warm glow of respect for the producer.

The after market

Favourite among ways to win good customer relations is looking after the customer once he or she has bought the product or service. We call this the after-market or after-sales service. Too often it is neglected. Do you worry about what happens after you've got the money in the till or the bank? Or are you like the second-hand car dealer who washes his hands of responsibility when the car he has just sold busts a big end on the motorway?

- Can your customers find spares or a good service agent easily?
- Do you train servicing engineers?
- Do you provide them with explanatory manuals or videos?
- Does the product carry an explicit, well illustrated service manual?
- If you provide a service, do you close down the account once the client has paid your fee?
- Is there a complicated guarantee with your goods, with infuriating exclusion clauses?

Some companies nowadays do not bother with smallprint guarantees but offer a general promise that if the product does not perform properly, it will be replaced or repaired, or a cash refund will be made. For many years, Marks and Spencer were able to sell clothes on this basis, without having changing rooms. A motor-car should work properly for several years, yet it is usually guaranteed for only a year which is surely an offence under the Fair Trading Act?

Taking care of the after-market can endear your customers to you, and result in both repeat purchases and recommendations.

Good customer relations thus depend on two major requirements:

- quality products or services
- responsible acceptance of after-market needs.

But we have discussed only the product and the after-sales service. What about the meat in the sandwich? How can PR techniques help you to achieve good or perhaps better customer relations? Don't be complacent because you are justly proud of your product or your servicing. In many world markets, the Japanese have walked over us because British manufacturers took it for granted that British was still best. To get an edge on competitors, national or international, it is the meat in the sandwich which counts, not the crusts which may have gone stale.

Some of this 'meat' is part of the marketing strategy which is only another way of emphasising the integral role that PR should, but does not always, play in the marketing mix. More about this in the next two chapters.

But whereas the good product brings out management philosophy in design and production, and the after-market reflects good marketing strategy, in between come the creative elements which depend on PR expertise. This is where you benefit from and exploit the skills of the PR consultant or the in-house PRO, and employ the specially created media of PR. Let us take a look at some of these methods.

Maintaining customer interest

One of the best ways to create customer satisfaction is to increase enjoyment of your product or service to make sure it is used, and to extend its uses. This can apply whether it is a sophisticated good like a sewing machine, camera or motor-car or something simple like flour, margarine, knitting wool or a garden aid. This can also be applied to services such as banking, insurance, hotels and restaurants, travel agencies and airlines.

You could just manufacture, distribute and advertise and leave it at that. But why stop there? Why not communicate with your customers by means of PR?

Printed matter

Many forms of print may be used, and you may even go into the publishing business and actually sell publications, or distribute them free or as sales promotion premium items. Knitting patterns, gardening books or pamphlets, road maps and tourist guides, cookery books and external house journals are all published by many companies. Some, like the Shell and Michelin guide books and maps, the McDougall cookery book and investment information digests like those from major brokerage firms are well-known examples. With the sophistication of desktop-publishing programs, even the small trader can produce a worthwhile publication to give away or sell.

Events

You may also find it valuable to organise events and activities which will bring you closer to your customers. The choice will depend on your business, and whether it is local, national or international. Some events can also produce the useful spin-off of media coverage. One of the tricks of PR is to gain an accumulative effect so that everything you do has an add-on opportunity or effect.

Visits

If your plant or operational centre is interesting, it may be a good idea to organise visits. For this you will need to plan a tour, have guides, provide refreshments, and have an exhibition, display or maybe a video or slide show. Visitors will also need something to take away such as a sample or gift and perhaps a presentation pack. Brewers, potteries, car makers, confectionery and food manufacturers do this. But so can local stores, banks, utilities, newspaper publishers, veterinary centres and other firms.

Visits can be organised in three ways. You can have an open day – or picnic as they have in the USA – when members of the community are invited. Visits can also be offered to groups such as clubs, societies, women's organisations and so on. A number of famous firms have arrangements with coach tour operators who make a business of selling coach party visits. Once organised, visits can be extended to trade buyers, and to the media as facility visits.

Showing the public – actual as well as potential customers – what you do when at work can encourage loyalty as well as broadening the people's understanding of manufacturing or servicing procedures. This has a useful knock-on effect when the visitor may later say to another something along the lines of: 'I always buy Heinz because I've been to their factory and seen how they make everything'.

Internet

Having a response page on your web site allows your customers to make comments to you about your products or services. Encourage positive comments by offering a token reward or a small discount to satisfied customers. Open a discussion group aimed at the Superwidget Owners Club – provide a forum for exchange of ideas and be ready yourself to contribute where problems arise or new angles are suggested. Be sure to keep your site thoroughly up-to-date with all the latest information and news.

Exhibitions

Participation in exhibitions can also bring you closer to your customers where you may be able to demonstrate production, either on the stand or by means of video. Or you may tour an exhibition in a special vehicle, or by train, or set it up in a hotel, library, civic centre or railway station concourse.

Meeting customers publicly can build good customer relations. Exhibitions also give you the opportunity to answer questions, give advice and hear opinions at first-hand. Such public confrontation helps to create confidence because there you are, face-to-face with customers you would never otherwise have met. Exhibitions may be primarily a sales and advertising medium, but they also have an important PR element.

Films and videos

Production of documentary films and videos, distributed on request or through a library, can be worth the investment if you make sure they reach significant publics. They can also be shown at customer and press receptions. This medium has been used by almost every kind of company, and there are valuable audiences all over the country which can be reached in this way. If you are an exporter, you can use the services of the Central Office of Information who distribute films and videos world-wide, often obtaining showings by foreign TV stations, but they must be free of advertising. Copies can also be placed with Visnews who offer an archival service to TV producers.

Some films of wide appeal may be accepted for showing in public cinemas, or on TV. It is also possible to sponsor a film or video on behalf of a charity, as has been done by makers of engines for life-boats or treatments for diabetics.

These productions may have a seemingly high production cost, and copies do have to be made, stored, serviced and distributed, but they can reach large, influential audiences. Provided the content does not date too quickly, the film or video can have a long life which can be extended if the master copy is capable of being up-dated. A special characteristic of films and videos is their entertainment value which helps to present a PR message very pleasantly.

Feature articles

A very inexpensive medium is the feature article. Customers can be told how to use or enjoy products or services by means of feature articles in newspapers and magazines. Provided they are of interest and value to a large number of readers, and are not infested with plugs, they will be welcomed by editors. But don't just send uninvited articles to editors. It is necessary to negotiate with appropriate editors, and produce what they want and supply it when wanted. Your PR consultant or in-house PRO can do this, or you may engage a freelance writer for the purpose. But, remember, an article is not just a long news release and (unless it is a syndicated article offered to non-competing journals) it is exclusive to one journal.

Without delving too deeply into techniques, the above suggestions provide a sample of what can be done to win or improve customer relations. These methods are different from and additional to advertising. They may suggest you can benefit from using professional PR talent. These suggestions may also show how you are sacrificing good or better customer relations simply because you are not exploiting the opportunities and methods which are available to you. Perhaps one reason why your customer relations are not as good as they might or should be is that your competitors *are* doing these things!

Although each PR activity may be different, it need not be isolated. This differs from advertising where it is most cost-effective to use the least number of media which give you the greatest market penetration. In PR, it is possible to be cost-effective by using the largest variety of media which reach as many different publics as possible, and duplication can be economical.

13

How Do I Educate the Market?

'We should constantly use the most common, little, easy words (so they are pure and proper) which our language affords.'
John Wesley

Had it ever occurred to you that your market needed educating? Or did you think that all you had to do was create a product or service and rely on a sales force and advertising to sell it for you?

No doubt if you presented your product or service to an advertising agency they would put together a suitable advertising campaign for you. It happens every day, and most of the new products or services that are launched turn out to be expensive flops – even when they have been test-marketed first.

It's not the fault of the advertising agency. It's the client's fault. The reason for most of the failures is that they were not understood by those who were expected to part with their money.

Take an extreme but typical example. Would all those millions of new investors have bought shares in privatised industries if the market had not been educated? Potential investors had to understand not only the business being privatised, but what share buying was all about. Much of the advertising was extravagantly wasteful.

Over the years there have been heavily advertised products which never took off, and the advertising was a financial loss. There have been others which only took off after the advertising failed, and a PR programme of market education was undertaken to the point when advertising could be reintroduced cost-effectively. One such instance was the Thoresen car-ferry which not even the travel trade understood in its first year of operation. Never forget your distributors!

Market education

There are two kinds of market education, and two kinds of market.

- One kind of market education **prepares the market in advance**, and it may take from six months to two years to do this. It is frequently overlooked by marketing and advertising people. If it is overlooked, advertising expenditure can be either or both excessive and useless. This kind of market education could be called pre-selling.

- The other kind occurs with **products and services that are already on the market**, and may be long established. Sales can be maintained, increased or even retrieved only if there is continuous market education. That means PR, not just advertising. In any case, PR costs less than advertising if you have something of interest and value to the public which the media will want to tell them about. It could be an ingredient for cooking recipes, a holiday venue, building society investments, a garden insecticide – anything, if knowledge of it is valuable to people.

There are also two kinds of market – the people who sell your product or service (**the trade**) and the people who buy it (**the consumers or users**). You cannot have one without the other, unless you are in direct response marketing. Some of the companies, products and services which have benefited from advance market education have been the Post Office, Findus Lean Cuisine, Rentokil, Sony, Thomson Holidays, The Independent, Concorde, and any number of new motor-cars which are no longer launched under a dust-sheet in showrooms. You might even include government leaks about impending legislation or policies, although it is arguable whether these so-called leaks are genuine leaks or events created by the government itself..

But to go back to the seven examples given above, we read about the new issues of postage stamps long before they are on sale; Lean

Cuisine had a six months PR launch before the posters appeared on London buses; Rentokil spent a year or more on PR before launching new services; the Sony camcorder had advance press notices long before it was on sale in the UK; Thomson Holidays launched their cheap holidays to Russia with press visits and reports by travel writers; and Concorde carried hundreds of important passengers on proving flights over the Atlantic before it went into service (was that really thirty years ago?).

Confidence has to be built up, curiosity and anticipation has to be induced, so that when launch day comes, sales resistance has been whittled away. This was not done with disaster products like New Smoking Mixture non-tobacco cigarettes, or the Sinclair C5 tricycle, nor was it done properly with the Millennium Dome so far as the public was concerned. Mind you, the final product has to match expectations, and the Dome failed to do this for many people.

One of the most important aspects of market education is winning over your distributors whether they be wholesalers, retailers, brokers or agents. Your own sales force is important in this respect too. It is too easy to assume that distributors will take stocks because of generous trade terms or the weight of advertising. Distributors are not just order takers and shelf fillers, not even in supermarket chains. They have to have faith in what they are selling, and very often they have to show evidence of this in their ability to advise customers.

There are many historical examples of this. Berger's Magicote paint was nearly a failure because hardware store sales people had no faith in the idea of a paint which needed no undercoat. Thoresen, in its first year in Britain, failed to convince travel agents that motorists could get to France and Spain via Southampton instead of the conventional Dover. Rentokil couldn't sell large cans of woodworm killer until they taught retailers the quantities required for different areas of infestation. Gas showrooms had problems in selling cookers fitted with timers until housewives learned their value. And New Zealand had to devote a great deal of effort to teaching the Japanese how to cook meat before New Zealand could sell mutton and lamb to an otherwise fish-eating nation.

The police introduced their Neighbourhood Watch scheme and

other prevention programmes through TV films. If a service like the police is to operate proficiently, this sort of 'market-education' by PR means is just as relevant as it is in the commercial world.

Similarly, the deregulation of the Stock Exchange (the Big Bang) was preceded by months of editorial explanation, and even before the Building Societies Act came into force, it was announced that certain societies intended to acquire estate agencies, even though this has subsequently proved to be a mixed blessing.

More currently, the advent of dotcom business was preceded by a welter of publicity and, since its explosion into the lives of the nation, it continues to receive countless explanatory articles, films, TV programmes and other messages telling everyone how wonderful it is and how everyone will benefit – even though a large percentage of the people do not know how and have not the means to access it.

> At a much smaller scale, some years ago an electrical dealer who wished to enter local government started to include a picture of his smiling face in all his shop adverts in local papers, some time before the scheduled election. Of course, when the election posters started to appear, everyone recognised mister nice-guy, the smiler, and he was duly elected. Clever!

This variety of examples shows that while market education or 'pre-selling' tactics are not widely adopted by the marketing and advertising fraternity, many organisations which appreciate the role of PR do in fact prepare the ground well and seek a favourable marketing situation well in advance of a launch. They do not merely rely on advertising as a panzer assault.

The effect of adopting a market-education strategy is fourfold.

- It helps to minimise sales resistance.
- It makes it easier for the sales force to achieve 'adequate distribution' prior to advertising.
- It helps to reduce the cost of advertising.
- It makes the advertising more effective because the market is already well disposed towards the product or service.

The techniques that can be applied are:

- a media relations campaign ranging over press, radio and TV as appropriate
- testing of prototypes by potential users – this often providing material for media relations
- production of slides, videos and other audio and visual aids for use at presentations to dealers, customers and the media
- works visits for dealers
- special campaigns aimed at particular opinion leaders or influential groups whose attitudes to the new product or service may be vital
- the production of printed material which may be needed to support these activities.

Has something very familiar occurred to you as a result of what you have now read in this chapter?

None of this can happen unless those responsible for its execution are privy to plans and policies at the earliest possible stage. In other words the PR consultant or in-house PRO **needs to be involved in decision making**, and that means being fully taken into the confidence of management. This is a very good argument for having an in-house PRO because she needs to be there, on the spot, helping you to make decisions and plans.

More than this, this advisory role is most valuable at the initial stage of product development. She is not there merely to send out a news release to coincide with the launch. Nor is it her job to pretend that a bad product is a good one, or to try to educate the market when it is too late.

Earlier in this chapter we said there were two kinds of market, the trade and the consumers. We have dwelt mostly on the consumer, but educating the trade is important. This applies whether your product or service can be explained to potential customers over a period, or whether it is one that does not permit a preparatory build-up. Many fast-moving consumer goods may have to be marketed quickly and secrecy may surround their development. The only permissible delay may be a test marketing programme, or zoned selling, before the national launch.

The field sales force will be greatly assisted if the wholesale *and* retail market are educated. This may be about the product itself, its application (requiring demonstration) or the advertising campaign. The tactics here could include:

- training sales staff
- providing sales people with counter-top demonstration units (e.g. slide, video)
- works visits
- dealer conferences with presentations of product and advertising
- receptions at TV studios where dealers are given advance showings of forthcoming TV commercials
- distribution of dealer magazines
- trade press receptions
- picture stories of the pack, stills from TV commercials, and details of media schedules for the trade press.

The PR campaign for dealers is a campaign in itself, and the trade press can be a launch pad. The approach is quite different from that used to educate consumers. You may be fighting for shelf space. Dealers are being asked to invest large sums of money. They have to be convinced not only that the product performs but that people will actually walk in the store and ask for it or take it off the shelf. For them, it is a gamble – good or bad business. It may put their reputation, livelihood and bank balance on the line. They may have had a bad experience with a previous product of yours or of a competitor. They may be nervous or sceptical and they will inevitably be greedy.

This is a very different proposition from the single customer who pays his money and takes a chance. For the retailer, it is only one of many products which he is being asked to stock. This can be very critical indeed for the buyer of a large chain of stores.

This kind of operation calls for teamwork on your side. Management, marketing, sales, advertising, production, transportation and PR are in this together.

And, as we shall see in the next chapter, it more than justifies the application of PR right through the marketing mix. It is a question of PR-mindedness, that is of putting yourself in the customer's or the dealer's shoes. Customer and dealer relations are bound up in market education. You are not just propagating your point of view, but trying to tell people what they need to know if they are going to respond to advertising and if they are going to buy. Otherwise there is no point in developing a new product or service in the first place, or in trying to maintain and develop the sales of an existing one.

14

How Does PR Relate to Marketing?

'Marketing is producing and selling at a profit
goods that satisfy customers'.

David Malbert

The late David Malbert, City Editor of the London Evening Standard, defined marketing succinctly. The marketing mix includes every element from the origin of the product or service to the after-market. Some of these elements, and their PR implications, have been discussed already.

How do you relate PR to marketing? Conventional marketing tends to regard PR as a separate, optional element, a part of marketing at best. Philip Kotler, whose books have influenced much of the teaching of marketing, hides PR under 'publicity'. This is one reason why marketing people tend to have a lowly picture of PR, virtually devaluing it.

Are you prepared to relegate PR to the marketing department where it may become little more than an optional extra, no more than product publicity to support advertising? Placed there, PR may be regarded in a derogatory fashion as no more than 'free advertising'. That is a perversion of PR, although very common.

Or do you see PR as a management function which services the entire organisation, of which marketing is only one very important section?

If you accept PR in this broader, more comprehensive way, its relation to marketing becomes more significant and practical. If you think of this aspect as marketing communications, PR becomes a vital part of the marketing manager's philosophy and concerns his whole thinking and strategy. Now, you are using PR in the sense of making every effort to understand distributors and consumers, and to communicate with them at every opportunity. We have already seen how this works with customer relations and market education.

PR clearly relates to many if not all the elements of the marketing mix when it has to do with overcoming hostility, prejudice, apathy and ignorance; with creating knowledge, understanding, goodwill and reputation; with establishing corporate identity and corporate image; and with effecting change of attitudes and behaviour.

In a book of this nature, it would be tedious to consider every possible element of the marketing mix for every kind of product or service, but there are some elements which are common to all of them. Among them are the name of the company or brand; the packaging; pricing; advertising; and sales promotion. In this chapter, these five elements of the marketing mix will be discussed from the point of view of PR involvement.

Company or brand name

Let's begin with the name of your company. Do you like it? Is it the best name you could possibly have? Is it well-known, does it identify your company and what it does? How was it conceived? Perhaps it was derived from the name of the founder like Ford, Pilkington or Hine. Or did it result from an amalgamation or merger? Perhaps it is an acronym like Fiat, Sabena or Toshiba which combines bits of very long business names. Perhaps it lends itself to familiar abbreviations or familiarisations like NatWest, Marks and Sparks. Or are you known and understood by initials such as IBM, KLM or BMW?

Naming a company can be crucial to corporate identity, corporate image, identification and understanding. Much of this depends on memorability. Some names mean little outside the company itself. They are not explicit. This is poor communication. A company name that does its job is elementary but significant public relations.

Are you therefore satisfied with your company name, or do you think there is a good reason for changing it?

It's not easy to change a name without causing confusion, or provoking doubts that the new name means something inferior. We have seen some confusing changes of name in the motor-car industry. Look for instance at the various, evocative names such as BMC, BL, MG, Austin-Rover, or Hillman, Rootes, Chrysler, Talbot, Peugeot – many of these now subsumed into international corporate names. Ford have been so lucky as to be able to perpetuate one name. British Airways is one thing but BA lacks the identity of BOAC and BEA.

Or you could have a name like AA which may stand for Automobile Association, Advertising Association or Alcoholics Anonymous. When you ask someone to ring the AA, does that person know which one you mean? Thinking to do you a favour, the wrong one could be contacted! Similarly, there are some acronyms which, when customers have had bad experiences, lead to unflattering inventions. Sabena has a pleasant sound, like a girl's name, yet there are passengers who interpret it as 'same awful bloody experience, never again'.

There is also the question of international usage. Some names, like Coca-Cola, are globally acceptable, but others have unacceptable connotations in other countries and different names have to be adopted. Rolls Royce opted not to use the name Silver Mist for one of its cars because it just would not sell in Germany – ask a German! Some names seem to have been created without considering their communication functions. Are they distinctive, easy to pronounce, memorable, promotable or internationally acceptable?

So, if you were creating a new name, either for your existing company or for a new venture, what sort of name would you choose?

There are some interesting possibilities, and some psychological factors, which are worth considering. Nowadays, we are seldom concerned about the name of the founder, unless perhaps it is a professional practice when the names of partners are more suitable. It could be a geographical or national name, which could be useful if the name of a town or city is characteristic of your industry, but it could be inhibiting if you want to operate nationally or internationally. But, as with the case of British Airways, British

Midland and British Caledonian, national identification could be very important.

It could be a made-up name or an acronym. Names with vowels are very effective and two, or better still three, syllables, as in Texaco, Yamaha or Nabisco and, with two syllables only, Omo, Oxo and Kodak.

It is best to avoid difficult names like Fyffes, Peaudoux or Hoechst which can be mispronounced or misspelt. The top 25 companies in the UK all have easily pronounced names (with the possible exception of Reuters). But clever names are Esso (which few people associate with Standard Oil), Elf (the French petrol, a name which was produced by a computer) and Amstrad (derived from Alan Minter Sugar TRADing).   Sets of initials (and again three are very effective) can absorb long forgettable company names and yet become synonymous with the company's business as with the ones already quoted, IBM, KLM and BMW. Everyone knows IBM make computers, KLM is the Dutch airline, and BMW is a quality German motorcar. Initials like EMI, GEC and TI are also used to precede divisional names. It is interesting that British Home Stores changed to BHS as part of a new image campaign. JCB is used as a generic name for earth-moving machinery and was derived from the initials of the founder.

Some surprisingly eccentric names have appeared, such as Apple, Fish and Egg, the online banking arm of Prudential (a serious and appropriate name). The dotcom arena has spawned some odd names as well as many which succinctly describe their purpose, such as goodideas.com or boozebypost.com.

Acronyms like Amstrad are excellent, and we have long grown accustomed to ones such as Fiat and Daf without being bothered about their derivation. Acceptability is often a main feature of acronyms. They are often pleasant-sounding and easy to remember. Choice of name for company, product brand, or a particular model or range is therefore a vital part of marketing communications. It is something on which PR consultancies and advertising agencies frequently advise, and it often pays to draw up a list of possible names and submit them to a research company. Some of the names with which we are very familiar were arrived at in this way.

An important reason for taking a lot of trouble over choosing a name is that it is difficult or unwise to change it, and you have got to live with it. Some changes seem to be quite baffling and not helpful in PR terms, such as the shift from Midland Bank (easy to remember and quite explicit) to HSBC which cannot be pronounced as an acronym and does not have any immediate meaning or recognisable industrial base. HSBC Holdings plc stands amongst the top ten banks in the world – all the other nine listed actually have the word 'bank' (or their national equivalent) in their name.

Sometimes a difficult situation occurs when a company expands by acquiring rival companies and is able to offer a comprehensive range of products or services in a certain field. Some of the names of these companies may also have less than attractive trading names. There was a company called Disinfestation Ltd which ran a pest control service. It was sometimes mistakenly called Anti-Disinfestation and even Disingestation!

The other companies in the group were called Chelsea Chemicals, Woodworm & Dry Rot Control, Rodine, Scientex Laboratories, Rentokil, Fumigation Services and so on. The holding company was called British Ratin. It was a mess of rather awkward-sounding names. Management took the wise decision of seeking a single name for the whole group. The company has never looked back since, after a painstaking and often agonising search for a new name, it settled on the one good name which it already possessed, Rentokil. The letter 'R' is often a good positive letter with which to begin a name. Rentokil also has three syllables and three vowels, making it a rhythmic name which is easy to pronounce, spell and remember.

The name also has an interesting origin, and subsequent change of possible meaning as a result of the emergence of other similar names. The founder of Rentokil, Professor Harold Maxwell-Lefroy of Imperial College, London formulated an insecticide in order to eradicate death watch beetle in the timbers of Westminster Hall in the 1920s. Following the success of this treatment, he decided to market bottles of the fluid and set up a company in 1927. As an entomologist, he called his product Entokil, based on the Greek entoma for insects, but when this proved unregistrable he added the letter 'R'. However, today, with so many names like Rent-a-van, many people think the name means 'rent to kill', which is probably no disadvantage! When the company went public, its single new name was an asset, and shares were well over-subscribed.

People sometimes wonder why ex-colonial countries change to strange-sounding names like Zimbabwe or Zambia, but they are very meaningful locally and spell national pride. Zimbabwe is a historical ruined city and Zambia has its Zambesi river. The new names are more meaningful than Rhodesia and Northern Rhodesia to the people of these countries and often act as rallying calls to the locals as witnessed in 2000 in Zimbabwe where the indigenous peoples tried finally to shake off the old imperial yoke.

Mergers have given rise to long names – especially in accounting and law – and a trend is to drop capital initials or ignore spaces in names, such as the September 1997 merger of Coopers and Lybrand with Price Waterhouse to create PricewaterhouseCooper or the equally 'spaceless' publishing house of HarperCollins.

On the other hand, names which are meaningful to their creators may mean nothing to strangers. How many people outside Indonesia realise that Garuda (the name of the national airline) is the name of a national bird, or that Volvo is derived from the latin volvere, the first person singular being volvo, 'I roll'. How many motorists associate Volkswagen with Hitler's 'people's car'? Or know that sanyo means three oceans? Racal sounds very 'electronic' but was actually taken from the names of the founders of the company, sir Raymond Brown and G. Calder Cunningham.

Names can have strange, unknown or forgotten origins, but if they measure up to the demands of a good name, as set out above, they will do their job admirably.

Packaging

We have already commented on how the convenience of packages can help to promote good customer relations, but how well do your packages communicate? They are not just pretty boxes, bottles or jars, asking to be taken off the shelf and popped into the trolley.

Of course, packages are designed for instant recognition and even to encourage impulse buying. Sales promotion schemes are also built into package design. But how well is goodwill – or ill-will – fostered by your packaging?

As well as the convenience factor, there is also the inconvenience factor. Waxed cartons are apparently very convenient for drinks, until you try to open one. Most airtight screw-top jars are a pain to open, especially if you have arthritis. Try opening one of those childproof tubs of tablets in the dark, when you have to match up the two arrows! And how do you know when an aerosol is about to run dry?

Every business has its own kind of packaging. Some insurance companies send you a policy on a slip of paper you could easily lose, others put it in a huge, mock-leather wallet that you don't know where to store. Lawyers are notorious for sending documents in a size that bears no resemblance to standard paper sizes. The travel agent packages airline tickets nicely in a handy wallet complete with luggage labels, but how many finger-nails have you broken trying to get batteries or screws out of blister-packs mounted on display cards?

A lot of packs are made for a purpose other than convenience – mainly retail display – and they provoke disappointment or dismay when the customer gets them home. We are fascinated by the big packets of garden seeds, with their glorious full-colour pictures. When we open the packet, it's like opening one of those Russian dolls. Way down in the corner of the packet is a minuscule packet just big enough to hold the five seeds inside. We thought we were buying about a hundred!

Some companies are now using 'anti-packaging', such as Tesco's Value range of products, which are shelved with very plain red-and-blue-on-white packs that do nothing intrinsically to attract buyers. However, in their own right and after much publicity, these instantly recognisable packs say this is a no-fuss product packed cheaply and therefore good value.

Are you one of the idiots who infuriates customers with damn-fool packages? Or do you apply that PR philosophy of thinking how you can please and help the customer? That's the way to build goodwill.

Packages often create a communication gap, when communication is all important. This can happen with the label or any part of the package – including a stuffer pushed inside a packet – which is supposed to give information. That information may involve essential advice. Have you seen the instruction sheet, eventually found packed in a plastic bag deep inside the polystyrene mouldings, that says, 'first open the main carton and remove the instruction sheet'? Brilliant!

There are some manufacturers, bless them, who do assume their customers are idiots. On a weedkiller, they write in big letters, 'Poison. Do not drink. It may kill you'. There are reliable domestic appliances which carry wiring instructions on the flex. On the other hand, there have been electric Christmas-tree lights arriving from the Far East which are lethal, with bare wires and poor construction.

Some packages carry warnings that frighten the life out of you like on those super-tough adhesives that will stick your fingers or lips together if misapplied. But some of the instructions are in such small print that you need a magnifying glass to read them, and they baffle anyone who is too vain to wear glasses. Some products get banished to the back of the cupboard because people cannot or will not be bothered to read the instructions. It's no use saying that it is their fault, because an unused product is one that does not give customer satisfaction, is not recommended, and is not bought again. That is bad PR, not only poor marketing.

If you buy a Sony portable television set, it comes in a large cardboard box, but there are gauze-covered slits for your fingers, and you can carry it comfortably. If you buy a suit or a large garment at Marks and Spencer, it is folded carefully and put in a big carrier bag that keeps it flat and uncrumpled. And if you buy glass or tableware, the shop assistant puts it in a cardboard box with a handle so that you can carry it without breaking anything. But why, when you purchase a CD-ROM, does it come in a box big enough to hold three pounds of chocolates?

Packaging is about care and caring for the customer.

Pricing

The price you charge for your product or service should be the one at which you expect to achieve your sales target. Basically, it will need to recover costs, unless you are buying your way into the market. It may also have psychological implications. Is it (a) what people expect to pay, (b) what they consider value for money, (c) worth the sacrifice of their money, (d) a bargain, or (e) does it imply prestige? These are all important aspects of pricing, and each has its PR as well as economic or psychological value.

Some organisations have built their reputations on their pricing policy. One firm of DIY stores has even called itself Payless, and a supermarket chain is called Pricerite. Although retail price maintenance was abandoned many years ago, price (even if only 'recommended' or 'list') features strongly in most advertising. Conversely, the most powerful single word in advertising is FREE, right down to Freepost, Freephone and Freenet.

People are naturally money and cost conscious. Nothing riles a person more than a press advertisement or direct mail shot which does not state the price.

After all, even a millionaire has a limited amount of cash, and not everyone goes mad with plastic money. One card company says most people do not incur interest on their accounts. You might say that the average customer is a greedy miser. But you want his or her money. We live in an exchange economy, not a something-for-nothing bonanza economy.

It is therefore a PR imperative that the price you charge – however reluctant may be the paying of it – is acceptable, producing no resentment, criticism or animosity. Shops which advertise that they will pay the difference if customers can buy the same goods cheaper elsewhere are staking their reputation on price. Their PR depends on it.

Does this surprise you? Did you think of price as just another element of the marketing mix, or are you seriously conscious of the customer satisfaction and goodwill towards your business that is bound up in price? This conversation was overheard in a shop.

Salesgirl: 'Two pounds ninety-five, please'.
Customer: 'It was only two pounds ninety last week!'

Five penn'orth of ill-will. Was it worth it? There was a similar irritated exchange over the price of a jar of coffee in an episode of EastEnders. The government may boast about inflation coming down but the shopper is still aware that it has never stopped going up! Not like the 1930s, when advertisers were always advertising lower prices for popular lines.

The price is only right if it what the purchaser deems to be fair and correct for the product or service. Too low and it is a cheap, tatty product – too much and it is a rip-off.

Advertising

The respectability of advertising seemed to be reasonably accepted until commercial television came along in Britain in the 1950s and suddenly people became aware of advertising and the enormity of its cost. They had to watch ads they didn't want to watch, whereas with press advertising they could ignore the ones that did not interest them. They did not appreciate that with mass-market FMCG, the amount of advertising cost per unit was infinitesimal. A new antagonism grew up towards advertising.

Then Shirley Williams, in her role as Secretary of State for Prices and Consumer Protection, demanded at the Advertising Association Conference in 1979 that voluntary advertising controls should have teeth. The Advertising Standards Authority took heed and ever since, members of the public have been invited to complain about any advertising they consider to be unethical. One teetotaller sent the ASA 150 complaints about alcoholic drink advertising.

Advertising is vulnerable. Any clown can complain to the ASA. If the complaint is investigated, irrespective of whether the complaint is upheld or rejected, it is reported for all and sundry to read in the monthly Case Report published and distributed by the ASA. Cases are then quoted in many newspapers and magazines. By just being in the

Case Report, a question mark is put against a reputable name. Before the advent of ASA, maligned advertisers sued for libel. Not now – it's publish and be damned – and it may be you who is damned.

In one issue of Case Report the following names appeared: Barclays Insurance Company, British Airways, British Gas, Eastern Electricity, The Electricity Council, Ford Motor Company, Framlington Unit Management, IBM (United Kingdom), Iberia Airlines, Imperial Chemical Industries, Jetsave Travel, Manchester International Airport, Nissan UK, Prudential Assurance, Scotcade, Southern Electricity, and under Sales Promotion: Alberto-Culver, Bejam Freezer, Calor Gas, Carlton Highland Hotel, Harveys, and Trans World Airlines. How are the mighty fallen – or are they? Of these 23 complaints, 17 were upheld and only six were not!

It is very bad PR to have one's advertising put on the block like that. Maybe, some of the things complained about were unintentional, or perhaps the copywriter was over-zealous. Nevertheless, it does mean that when you use advertising, it must be beyond reproach.

Benetton pushed the boundaries as far as they could with ads that contained images of new-born babies and condemned murderers – nothing whatever to do with their product lines – but it did get their name seen by a lot of people. It is a moot point whether the people who actually complained about these ads helped or hindered Benetton's PR efforts. It certainly made the company appear innovative and different in many people's eyes.

When you advertise, you go naked into the arena. You stake your reputation on what you say. There is nothing more public than advertising. The days of Barnum should be over.

Remember the adage, already quoted, that advertising is what you say about yourself, PR is what other people say about you. Make sure that the two match, because the one can influence the other.

'Guinness Is Good For You' was true all the time 'you' meant the consumer. The 'Ultimate Driving Machine' is grand provided it does not ultimately break down or wallop into the back of your Jag. Remember when in 1990, The Labour Party did not get very far with its Yesterday's Men election campaign, and British Rail got a resounding raspberry for We're Getting There?

Beware, then, of the advertising wizards who may conjure up a magical campaign that may look the cat's whiskers – or is it only a rabbit? Run, rabbit run, may be your slogan when the campaign rebounds on you. Then, you may relish the old Chinese saying:

> *'There are thirty six ways of dealing with a problem;*
> *the best one is to run away.'*

Sales promotion

Here we have another accident-prone element of the marketing mix. There has been a terrific boom in sales promotion, and some of its pundits reckon it is more cost-effective than PR. Some people go too far and regard it as a kind of PR. It does have PR implications, good ones and bad ones.

Sales promotion certainly takes you into the market place, and brings you closer to your customers. But there are cherry pickers, shoppers who go round the supermarkets buying only the special offers and playing havoc with brand loyalties.

The current tendency is to run schemes which can be completed at the point of sale without putting the customer to the trouble of having to post coupons, tokens or cash. The old 'self-liquidating' premium offers have been largely superseded by on-pack offers, High Street redemption schemes, gifts supplied via distributors (e.g. petrol stations) and with on-the-spot prize competitions like scratch cards. Some of them produce fun for the customers, others have a bargain appeal, and often they are allied to what was said above about price.

Satisfaction is important. If the customer is disappointed, has to wait a long time to receive a premium offer, or the offer is over-subscribed and only a cash voucher is received, ill-will is easily provoked. In the past, a number of schemes went sour simply because a brand manager under-estimated demand or the ability of a supplier to deliver in volume quickly.

If you are contemplating a sales promotion scheme, think of its long term effect on goodwill and reputation as well as its short-term effect on sales, profits and brand share.

There is also the retailer to consider. Is he enthusiastic about the scheme, or is its handling a nuisance to him? Does the extra trouble compensate for extra trade?

And don't forget the perils of mis-redemption. It may be pointless to have a cash voucher offer which, in spite of all your threatening wording, will be redeemed by Sainsbury's against purchase of any other product they stock. There are bright shoppers who laugh at your schemes and go on a shopping spree with a clutch of money-off vouchers. All you are doing is giving money away, and the supermarket chains are just as delighted as the happy housewives.

The trade can be easily offended if a company makes a special offer or gift of a product which the same trade also sells. An example might be if a lamp shade manufacturer gave away free electric light bulbs. One such instance proved disastrous all round.

A large British company bought a certain product at £1 each and ran a self-liquidating offer of this product at £1 plus tokens from packs. It spent £1 million on the purchase of these products, but in a very short time received two million applications ! This meant it had to spend another £1 million to honour applications. The scheme deprived the trade of the sale of this type of product since the public could now buy it so cheaply. Worse still, one of the principal manufacturers of this kind of premium product went bankrupt because of the collapse of retail sales.

You may believe you have a corporate image of a splendid company which produces – at a profit – goods or services your customers want and enjoy. Or is your fond image at the mercy of unpronounceable, forgettable names, thoughtless packaging, irritating pricing, near-the-knuckle advertising and annoying sales promotion schemes? In other words, is narrow-minded marketing your PR undoing – or is the strategy so PR-minded throughout, that your corporate image is once again enhanced?

15

How Do I Deal with Opinion Leaders?

'Ignorance, madam, pure ignorance.'
Samuel Johnson

Opinion leaders are all those people whose opinions are listened to with respect, and who are believed to know what they are talking about. The world is full of oracles: from parents, teachers, parsons and politicians to writers and broadcasters who are regarded as experts. It may be that they know more and more about less and less.

They can be dangerous or indispensable. They can help or hinder. We have only to consider court cases to see how expert witnesses can confound one another. Try to find a proper definition of public relations in any dictionary and you won't find many. The Compact Oxford English Dictionary has a fair attempt with 'the professional maintenance of a favourable public image by a company etc.' but few lexicographers seem to understand the subtleties. 'Favourable' here does not equate with the idea put forward at the start of the book of 'mutual understanding' although that in itself would be favourable.

When asked why, in his dictionary, he defined 'pastern' as the 'knee' of a horse, Dr. Johnson replied 'Ignorance, madam, pure ignorance'. (To save you looking it up, it is actually between the fetlock and the hoof!) You may well have to deal with opinion leaders who are less frank or honest.

Opinion leaders can be a funny lot because their authority is at stake, and to be proved wrong is to be found out. Pride may dislike truth.

You and your business are surrounded by opinion leaders. A doctor once treated a colleague for two weeks for gout. A second doctor cured him of a bruised heel. So much for expert opinion.

Opinion polls are as fickle as Stock Exchange prices, as we frequently see with the month-by-month fortunes of political parties and party leaders.

There are some people who believe that public relations is about creating a favourable climate of opinion. They must be joking. Opinion is not something that can be generalised because it is personal, and this is the problem when dealing with opinion leaders.

In order to deal with opinion leaders, they have to be identified, and the validity of their opinions, and the effect of their opinions upon the organisation, need to be evaluated. It could be that they do not matter, or are unlikely to be influential; on the other hand, it may be a vital public relations task to see that opinions of certain people are fairly expressed and are based on correct information. Opinions can be like rumours whose origins are difficult to trace and whose spread is difficult to check.

The first step is to identify all the kinds of people who do express opinions which may affect your business. The list may be formidable, and perhaps it's a job you have never thought of doing before. Do it now! Never let corrections go by default.

Then it pays to find out what these opinions are. You may need to carry out an opinion survey for this purpose. Or you may have sufficient feedback by way of customers' complaints, salesmen's reports, published or broadcast statements to know what is being said. The chances are that until you actually identify your opinion leaders, you will not take the next step of finding out what they are saying. There may be reasons for suspecting that negative opinions exist. Sales may have fallen, share prices may have slipped, dealers may not be stocking up. Why? What have people been saying?

Not all opinion leaders are broadcasting their opinions in the media; there can be an undercurrent of subversive animosity which needs to be identified and eliminated.

When there are identifiable individuals whose opinions are

misinformed, one of the best tactics is to confront them face-to-face. They can be visited, invited to the office or factory, taken out to lunch but in one way or another encouraged to meet you and discuss the subject. It is surprising how such friendly confrontations can turn enemies into friends.

In chapter 6, we looked at the possibility of someone slagging you off on the internet. This can be done in several ways.

- You may discover the existence of a mock-you site which is clearly intended to foment discontent. This might be called by a name rather like yours, for example, someone upset by McIntosh Medicines may open a site called quackintosh.com

- More dangerous to your activities would be a site called killerintosh.com, clearly the centre of uncontrolled venom against you.

- Less dangerous but still a considerable irritant would be a discussion group quietly undermining your company's prestige.

In any circumstance like these, you will need to become involved in order to set the record straight. Try to use the power of the site to your advantage. Always be honest, open and polite. You may be able to de-fuse the situation.

Sometimes, ill-disposed opinions arise because of ignorance and lack of information. It may be your fault that you've never bothered to tell them the true story. This, of course, is what a great deal of public relations is all about: making sure that the facts about your business are well-known. Your web site is a great place to do this.

If your opinion leaders are many and widely dispersed, you will have to select media which will reach them. This may not be possible through the mass media and you may find it necessary to produce special media which can reach them. External house journals, facts books, touring exhibitions, videos, presentations, receptions and seminars may be used.

Let's look at a few examples. Banks need to recruit school-leavers, but young people sometimes think of banks as dull places in which to work. As part of its staff recruitment programme, some time ago, Lloyds Bank produced a video for schools. It is a very entertaining and light-hearted production in which David Bellamy visits a branch of Lloyds and meets the surprisingly young staff and learns what they think about working in a bank.

This Lloyds Bank film takes the bull by the horns very nicely, and confronts opinion leaders who may be teachers or sixth formers with an enlightening picture of banking as a career.

Your distributors can be important opinion leaders. What do they say about your company or your products? Are they flattering or critical? Do they create customer confidence? Again, PR tactics can be employed. You may be able to organise dealer visits to your plant, or invite them to regional conferences. Another method is to distribute an external dealer house journal. Whatever the method, the need is to communicate with them in a way which is interesting, helpful and convincing.

The same applies to public figures and celebrities who make public statements about you. Take the 'insider dealing' scandals which broke in New York and London in 1986. It did not take long for opinion leaders from MPs to journalists to start making adverse comments about the City. Here was great need for the leaders of financial houses to meet these critics and make sure the criticisms were levelled at culprits, not the whole financial business. But on the whole, the financial leaders adopted a wagon-circle attitude and held their fire.

Many opinions are expressed in readers' letters to the press, and readers' letter columns make very popular reading. Answering or correcting such letters can be another way of reaching a great variety of opinion leaders. They may represent organisations which have opinions to express about your business or industry, or individuals whose comments may influence the opinions of others.

There are three problems here. Readers' letters appear in countless newspapers and magazines, many of which you may never see. How do you keep track of what all these writers are saying about you? If you do reply, there is no guarantee that the readers of the original letter will necessarily read yours. And the editor may not print your reply. The second is a risk you have to accept, but there are possible solutions to the first and third problem.

You can establish a system of monitoring the press. A press cutting agency can be engaged to clip letters of interest to you, but the agency must be properly briefed on what you are looking for. You can also instruct members of your staff, including members of the field sales force or branch managers, to scrutinise the press for letters that need answering. Careful briefing is necessary in both cases because writers may not necessarily refer to your company or its brands by name. Criticisms might be of 'unit trusts', 'health drinks', 'packaged holidays', or 'man-made fibres' and still be relevant to your business and worthy of a reply.

A number of complaints and even legal actions have been mounted by companies which have suffered from bias or false statements made by the media. There have been examples of reckless or dishonest publishing and broadcasting. They have been investigated by the Press Council, the Independent Broadcasting Authority, the Broadcasting Complaints Commission and other authorities. There has been litigation, and some of it has taken five years to get cases into court. Maybe these efforts have had a warning effect, but they have hardly put the frighteners on the offending writers or producers.

How much better to retaliate instantly, as we have seen when companies heavily criticised by programmes such as Watchdog have produced replies in humourous song and verse. The best way to defend is to attack, and if the heat can be reduced by ridicule or maybe an amusing apology, this is better than demanding your rights. There is nothing like turning an enemy into a friend.

Dealing with opinion leaders can be done either individually or en masse. If there are important individuals who have got it wrong about your organisation, it may be a good plan to pick them off one by one in face-to-face meetings and try to convert them, or at least make them better informed. It is surprising how the personal touch can work miracles. Companies tend to be faceless monolithic things but people are people. Here are a few examples.

A woman journalist and author was writing damaging pieces about a certain make of domestic equipment. She was invited to visit the factory where the designer hosted her. He succeeded in changing her mind by pointing out that in order to drive her car away from the kerb she had to go through a much more complicated procedure than using the controls on the equipment she was criticising. End of criticism.

A new food product was being wrongly classified by food writers when in fact it was an alternative with certain health benefits. Instead of holding a traditional press conference the makers (through their PR consultancy) invited journalists to bring their partners to a dinner party at a London hotel. On arrival they were welcomed with a drink. Then they were assembled for the showing of a film about the origins and manufacture of the product, and its success in the country of origin. After this came a tasting session, followed by the opportunity to question a panel of company representatives. This was followed by a pleasant dinner-dance. Finally, as the guests left, they were invited to take home a sample. It was a very nice low-key occasion which resulted in excellent media coverage, and the end of the false notions about the nature of the product. The product has since become so popular that two other companies now market their rival versions.

A quango, intended to help a certain industry, was failing to get the support of industrial leaders who resented official interference. The director invited each leader to meet him for breakfast, lunch or at his or their office. The result was that he succeeded in getting these important people to form an advisory committee to help him with the project.

The editors of a group of trade magazines were hostile to one of the biggest companies in their trade. As a result of lunches being arranged for each editor which were hosted by the managing director of the company and his PR consultant, the situation was reversed. The problem was talked over amicably, and the editors adopted a much fairer attitude towards the company.

These are examples of face-to-face confrontation with critical opinion leaders, but when the opinion leaders are more numerous and scattered nationwide or throughout the community or across the internet, the overall PR campaign may have the objective of informing opinion leaders at large. This is where media relations, videos, external house journals, educational literature, seminars, mobile exhibitions and possibly sponsorships may be among the means of reaching them.

This emphasises the educational nature of public relations, and it is a good example of how PR differs from advertising. It is also a good example of how PR can augment advertising in the sense that advertising can be ineffective and wasteful expenditure if it is likely to be nullified by widespread antagonistic opinions.

We shall deal with research in Chapter 21, but here it is worth mentioning that in order to assess the extent of adverse opinions, an opinion poll can be conducted. This research can be repeated after efforts have been made to correct misinformed opinions so that the extent of the shift of opinion can be measured.

16

How Do I Handle Financial Relations?

'I cried all the way to the bank.'

Liberace

A quick answer to the question asked by this chapter is to appoint a specialist financial PR consultancy of which there are more than a score, mostly operating in the City of London. Their names and addresses will be found in the Hollis Press and Public Relations Annual, or information about many of them may be obtained from the Public Relations Consultants Association. There is also the City and Financial Group of the Institute of Public Relations, which consists of individuals engaged in financial PR.

However, there are things you can do yourself, and aspects of financial relations such as communications with your shareholders, announcing interim and annual trading results, producing the annual report and accounts, and the organising of the annual general meeting, which you can handle internally. Here are other activities for which your in-house PR department can be responsible.

The Stock Exchange not only has its own rules regarding the distribution of financial information and its systems such as SEAQ and SETS, but publishes a useful booklet on these topics, plus details about the admission of securities to listing. Details of listings can be obtained at www.listings.co.uk. General information about the Stock Exchange can be found by visiting www.londonstockexchange.com.

The IPR publishes a useful booklet, Guideline No 4, on the use, misuse and abuse of embargoes which specifically ban the broadcasting by any means whatever of information before a stipulated release date.

How well do you communicate with your shareholders? Today, shares are not only held in large blocks by institutions, or bought frequently as institutions have to invest incoming funds, or by speculative buyers, but by a growing number of small investors. In addition, an increasing number of employees now possess, or are encouraged to buy, shares in their own companies. Shareholders are therefore a rapidly growing PR public.

Do you keep in touch with all these people, and why should you do so? Remember, the smaller shareholders and your own employee shareholders are likely to be more permanent and less likely to 'play the market'. They will be less familiar with share buying, share selling, PE ratios, and the significance of both share prices and dividends. These things are very different from holding a building society account.

As the number of your shareholders grows, your communication responsibilities increase. Uninformed, confused or disillusioned shareholders could have a disastrous effect on the stability of your company. Imagine what would happen if thousands or only hundreds of your shareholders thought the company was doing badly, or they disliked your policies or even your products? What would they do? It would be like a run on a bank. Not for them the shrewd investor's rule that when they run you walk, when they walk you run. Their reaction would be the reverse. They would run all the way to their bank manager to sell their shares. They really would cry all the way to the bank.

It does not even take a mass revolution of shareholders or other interested people to cause havoc. There are a number of examples of small groups of carpetbaggers who have excited interest in such matters as the demutualisation of building societies and have been so effective that the directors have changed tack. The debate within the Bradford and Bingley in mid-2000 was one such, this in spite of the very successful flotations of such giants as the Halifax and Norwich

Union in 1997 and others later on.

Similarly, if employees lost confidence in you as an employer, if they even went so far as to seek jobs elsewhere, they would not want to own your shares any more. If they lost their jobs, they would sell up.

The forces of supply and demand would apply on the Stock Exchange, and your share price would fall. If there were big sales, your share price could plummet, especially if the institutional buyers got worried by your falling share price. The predators would be alerted. You could be facing a take-over bid.

You may need to think about any minefields you may have sown in your business through employee share ownership. You may have to get your skates on to keep the company punters happy. They were brought up on football pools, and there is a difference between gambling with pennies and locking up hundreds of pounds. You have to explain this to them. They may not be the lucky employees who bought £200 of shares in the National Freight Corporation which became worth £7000 in five years.

We are back to the PR objectives of understanding, goodwill, and confidence which are based on knowledge. You have to keep your shareholders informed, not just when things are booming and you want to congratulate them on their wisdom in being on your share register. In fact, when things are difficult the need to communicate with shareholders is even more necessary.

The simplest way to communicate with them is by letter, but this can be made even more informative with an occasional newsletter. They may well be flattered to receive messages from the chairman of a big corporation.

Employees can be reached through the house journal which should contain financial news if many employees are shareholders. Again, an occasional letter from the chairman is a good idea.

Has it ever occurred to you how little your shareholders (including your employees) know about your business? You know it all (or maybe even you don't know everything), but their knowledge of your trading operations could be minimal. Many shareholders are amazed at how seldom they ever hear from the companies who depend on their money. Why should they have to rely on snippets in the city page of the daily newspapers? Your company may not even be quoted in the abbreviated city prices in the more popular papers.

Nowadays, even fairly popular newspapers have city pages, and your smaller shareholders are likely to read what city editors have to say. Press relations should not be confined to the FT. They can also read share prices on their television screens or on the web.

The same considerations apply to the annual report and accounts. The readership is likely to increase as more people become shareholders, perhaps through the new personal investment schemes. Reports need to be written succinctly, figures set out intelligibly and not too formidably for people unused to reading balance sheets. Charts will help to show what has happened to income, expenditure and profits.

A lot of annual reports are over-elaborate and unintelligible and this has been said in the business and financial press by people you would expect to understand their intricacies. A number of house journals do present annual results very attractively, even to non-shareholder employees who are entitled to understand a company's fortunes.

Several companies produce videos in which the chairman is interviewed about the report and accounts, and figures are explained by means of charts or animation. The video can be used in several ways. It can be screened at annual general meetings when there is a large attendance of shareholders; it can be offered to or sent to shareholders who do not attend the meeting; and it can be shown to staff at all your operational locations.

Another way of communicating with staff is by PC and e-mail. This could be an excellent means of communicating urgent news.

Financial PR is all about confidence, a precious asset which can be lost if you are not candid. True, financial information can be very sensitive, but it is mostly sensitive when there is something to hide. Frankness does not mean encouraging insider trading, and we are mostly concerned here with encouraging people to keep shares and neither buy nor sell them in difficult situations.

When things are normal, or trade and prospects are good, there is of course every justification for telling shareholders the good news. Here is an opportunity to spread more equity among employees.

Yet another problem is the speed with which stock market news is being communicated, such as by the London Stock Exchange's SEAQ system of automated quotations which have taken dealings away from the trading floor and the openness of dealing via the SETS order book. Similar systems exist on Wall Street and elsewhere. But not only is information distributed rapidly by computers, but it has been internationalised by means of satellite, and shares are being sold simultaneously in places like London, New York, Frankfurt, Paris, Amsterdam and Tokyo. Joint ventures have been proposed between London, Frankfurt and Nasdaq in America, for example, with a common trading service.

New services and approaches are constantly being introduced and this is where a professional advisor can help with keeping up to date. For instance, electronic auctions have been introduced to the SEAQ market and groupings such as techMARK (in November 1999) and extraMARK (in February 2000) opened up new areas of interest that attract both investors and companies.

We have looked first at two areas of change and growth in the money market. Now let us turn to the more traditional share buyers, the institutional buyers who are active in the stock market, looking for good investments. They include banks, insurance companies, pension funds and unit trusts. Their big purchases help to keep your share price healthy.

How well do their financial advisers understand your business? There have been cases in recent years when companies and their trading operations have been imperfectly understood. Again, this can be disastrous, and it's all down to good communications. This is where you may need the professional advice of a financial PR consultant. Investor relations has become a consultancy speciality.

In the City, there are special kinds of opinion leaders who need to be cultivated. That does not mean wining and dining them, although it can be done in a civilised way provided you are forthcoming with information.

A typical PR activity is the detailed briefing of investment analysts, those people who write and circulate researched reports on whether your company is a good or bad investment.

They may not always get it right, and that's to your disadvantage. Why do they not always get it right? Because you have not made sure that they have the facts that do you justice.

This is rarely secret or sensitive information but straightforward information about the nature of your business. Analysts may quite wrongly think you are in a high risk business, have weak management, lack marketing skills, are too diversified, have interests in the wrong countries, and one way or another write you off as a sound investment. If you can put the record straight, do so!

This sort of PR is, once again, totally unlike advertising. If you appear too ecstatic, these wily people will think there's a rat to smell. So, if the briefing is done quickly in the boardroom or over lunch as a straight presentation of the situation, the experts can analyse it at face value.

Since the Big Bang, the Stock Exchange has become ultra vigilant about financial information and its givers. Regarding the release of financial news through third parties (e.g. PR consultancies) the Stock Exchange is very particular about confidentiality, always being worried about insider trading or the undue influencing of share prices. The Stock Exchange recommends that companies should exercise caution in appointing advisors or agents and the importance of their role should be made clear to any third party involved in the preparation and release of information on behalf of a company. They add that the responsibility for the failure of an appointed agent to ensure that the release procedures are adhered to rests solely with the company. In the event of continuing breaches of procedure, The Stock Exchange would request the company to review the appointment of the particular agent.

In terms of general information about quoted companies, the Share Monitoring Service can be accessed (once you have accepted the conditions of use of the site) at www.prism.londonstockexchange.com.

The Stock Exchange is so concerned about protecting its reputation that, in the case of a PR practitioner being investigated, it insists on doing so itself. It will not leave this to, say, the disciplinary procedures of the Institute of Public Relations.

Nevertheless, the Public Relations Consultants Association, which is made up of corporate consultancy members instead of the individual membership of the Institute of Public Relations, has adopted its own code regarding such sensitive topics as insider trading. It sets out some guidelines.

A member firm shall not misuse information regarding its client's business for financial or other gain. Nor shall it use insider information for gain. A consultancy, its members and staff shall not directly invest in their clients' securities without the prior written permission of the client and of the member's chief executive, chief financial officer or compliance officer.

PRCA members are asked to write a confidentiality clause into their employment contracts on 'price sensitive' share dealings and to explain the gravity of acting upon this information both from the point of view of the individual and from the reputation and professionalism of the consultancy.

The situation is not helped by a conflict between traditional financial PR and the demands of a business which has been dramatised by massive privatisation flotations, mega-mergers (and, in cases such as Guinness and Distillers, an aftermath leading to the downfall of business and financial leaders), deregulations, the Big Bang, de-mutualisations, new building society legislation and the flurry of new financial services and their marketing.

Traditional financial PR tended to be discreet. It is foolish to panic the volatile Stock Exchange. It is not like product publicity for popular consumer goods. Too much publicity could be bad for you.

But then came all the take-over bids and other financial games mentioned above, and they (subject to the Competition Commission and other attempts at control) depended on strident publicity. Much of the promotion has been utterly stupid and confusing, and has done the reputation of some major institutions and corporations no good at all.

Nevertheless, all these modern financial activities need more than frenetic advertising. They have to be understood, and so we are back to public relations. In a bewildering world where building societies turn overnight into banks, insurance companies sell shares, and stores like Marks and Spencer become licensed deposit-takers, it may not be too much to expect that our friendly Mecca bookmaker will soon be selling Premium Bonds. Especially if the government decides to sell off the Post Office!

But it does mean that while take-over bids may be the heady stuff of big business, hundreds of smaller and often High Street businesses concerned with money will have to communicate pretty clearly with an increasing number of people not normally concerned with such transactions. Moreover, this sort of business will be conducted either by strangers or by firms who were better known for something else. We shall also have the one-stop money supermarkets which will combine all sorts of allied services, such as house buying, mortgages and insurance. The possibilities of conducting such business on the web is already with us with an explosion of financial services now available at the touch of a button, right in your living room.

Finance can be a PR quagmire, but if it is neglected, your company could go out of business and you could be out of a job. And if your business is the kind that is taking on new financial services, it is going to be very necessary to show that you deserve to be respected and trusted. People are now menaced by all kinds of cowboys who seek to turn their dubious activities into profit-making exercises, no matter who they may cause to fall by the wayside as they travel on.

17

HOW CAN POLITICAL PR
HELP ME?

'Man is by nature a political animal.'

Aristotle

Few businesses are unaffected by politics, whether there is a large measure of state control, the economy is thrown more and more on the mercies of market forces, or there is consensus government.

All manner of government interference such as economic policies, taxation, import controls, consumer protection, privatisation, or the investigations conducted by select committees and Royal Commissions all affect many businesses, including yours.

What business is not affected in some way by the government's policies (or lack of them!) regarding education, health, social services, roads, railways or maybe security on the internet?

Does your business try to thrive or survive so far as it is permitted by the government of the day?

Some businesses have succeeded because they have assiduously maintained a dialogue with government, irrespective of the party in power.

An important facet of democratic government is that it discusses its plans and proposed legislation with those most likely to be affected. In this way, our legislators can benefit from discussions with representatives of the industry, profession or interest concerned. Trade associations, voluntary bodies, professional associations, trades unions and other bodies are invited to make representations. They are the pressure groups which provide links between special interests and the government.

In this way, government can deal with a few representative people when it would be impossible to talk to the multitude and get their decision, except perhaps by plebiscite. This is not unlike the industrial situation where it is simpler to negotiate with trade union representatives than with the whole staff as individuals.

So, one way in which you can apply political PR is by supporting a body which represents your interests to government and to individual politicians of all parties. Apart from dealing directly with ministries, there can also be lobbying of MPs. On many issues there are usually groups of MPs who form 'the lobby' on, say, motoring or farming or other subjects which particularly interest them.

It may, therefore, be very important that you keep informed and even meet and know the MPs who are especially interested in your subject and need to be kept informed about what you do. A quick search through Dod's Parliamentary Handbook will show you the principle interests of MPs and members of the Lords.

Do you know who they are? If you do not, don't blame them for being uninformed and for acting against you out of ignorance. For that matter, do you know what they say about your business or industry in the House, in committees, at political meetings or even on TV programmes like Any Questions? They, too, are opinion leaders. Political PR, or parliamentary liaison as it is often called, is not only about communicating with Members of the Houses of Parliament, and with the senior civil servants who advise ministers. It is also about knowing what goes on in Parliament, including what is about to happen if it has to do with your business.

This is where you can benefit from engaging one of the specialist parliamentary liaison consultancies. According to the brief you give them, they will monitor Hansard and other reports on your behalf, and keep you aware of the procedures of Parliament regarding White Papers, Green Papers, committee stages of bills, debates, select committees and Royal Commissions, investigations by the DTI or the Competition Commission and when new legislation becomes effective.

Many of these parliamentary occasions can provide opportunities for you to inform MPs or to submit evidence, thus protecting your interests by getting proposals amended or dropped. It does, of course, depend on the style of government. One may believe in a trinity of government, industry and unions – others will not. The turn of the last century saw a very different style of government from the preceding Conservative years, and coalition and consensus may depend on communication with business.

We are part of Europe so your business may be affected by the EU and the European Parliament, or by the need to harmonise legislation among individual EU countries.

For example, one food ingredient was listed as a chemical by the food laws in several European countries. This meant that this ingredient was illegal in countries like Germany which were large potential markets. The company's PRO conducted high-level PR work, presenting dietary reports to food ministers, until eventually country by country, the legislation was changed. As a result, the company gained millions of pounds' worth of new business in EU countries. Since the company was a European multi-national with its HQ in Brussels, this political PR effort was vital to its trading success in many countries.

International politics may therefore be vital to your business, but they may range world-wide if you are an exporter faced with foreign import restrictions, special requirements concerning ownership of foreign-based subsidiaries, licensing, taxation and duty laws. You may have to work closely with the DTI, international chambers of commerce, foreign trade missions, foreign embassies and their commercial attaches, and other quasi-political bodies like those which advise on and arrange links with overseas markets.

At the smaller end of the spectrum, you may need to keep abreast of local politics and the machinations of your parish council. The decisions that are taken at local level – do we site the new supermarket here or there? will the new ring-road lessen casual trade? – can substantially affect your business. Lobbying can equally take place at parish level as it can in Brussels. Local chambers of trade or associations of town traders can wield quite a lot of influence and you would be well advised to join in with such formations – or at the very least, watch the local press and try to gauge trends and changes in your locality.

What about the political parties themselves? In Britain we do not have that American peculiarity, the political action group (PAG), of which scores exist representing different pressure groups which are financed by industry. But we do have a variety of political parties with very different attitudes as to how the country should be governed. You may find that it will pay to explain your business to parties with which you do not personally agree. Surely, every party should understand each and every industry and the separate firms that it comprises?

Almost any legislation is bound to favour some and harm other business interests. You can avoid being a victim only if you express your views to those who influence decisions. As we saw with Sunday trading, it is possible for those with very definite views to make a government look very foolish. Governments are just as much at your mercy as you are at theirs.

In political PR, it is therefore a waste of time putting your head in the sand or relying on a contribution to the funds of your favourite party. There is no guarantee that the party you finance is going to help you, if only because governments have to deal with scores of conflicting issues, and you are always going to be on one side or the other and never always on the government's. Each issue has to be dealt with separately and on its own merits as far as you are concerned.

One company may want quotas of Japanese imports raised, another will want them lowered; one may want money spent on improved roads, another on improved health services; one may want improved training facilities, and another will demand better postal or telephone services.

What are your political demands and objectives? Have you defined them, or do you just put up with things? Do you have a positive political programme, or are you just in love with the government? They say we have the government we deserve.

Your business is bound to be affected by politics and it is essential that you identify how, when and why political action – at home and abroad – is going to help or harm you. Then you need to plan what you are going to do about it.

- Do you include political PR as part of your in-house PR programme?

- Do you hire a specialist political PR consultancy?

- Do you identify the MPs and councillors who take a special interest in your subjects (and not just your trade or industry), and how do you plan to lobby them?

- Which ministries or local government departments should you approach through civil servants ?

- Do you need to go higher, and make approaches to the prime minister and to cabinet ministers? Locally, do you approach your council chairmen or the chairs of relevant committees?

- Can politicians be reached through the media they are most likely to read or see?

- Do you write letters to MPs or councillors, or send them literature including perhaps your house journal or annual report and accounts?

- Do you invite your local political bigwigs to visit your plant, or maybe ask an all-party group to make such a visit?

- Do you belong to and take an active part in associations which can represent you politically? They can send delegations to see ministers, prepare reports for politicians to read, and present evidence to government committees or quangos. You could be one of the spokesmen on a delegation.

You may be able to direct or conduct some of this yourself but if politics matter in your business, the advice of a specialist consultant could be a worthwhile investment. Even in a democracy, government is about power and staying in power, and not about looking after your interests.

18

What Can I Do About Community Relations?

'Good fences make good neighbours.'

Robert Frost

Does it matter what your neighbours say about you or do you care? Or do you believe that public relations starts on the doorstep?

The people who live (or work, shop or visit) in the vicinity of your premises or plant can be your friends or your enemies. They can include actual or potential customers or employees. They matter. You ignore them at your peril.

Some people are so busy making products that are sold on the other side of the world, that they think their affairs are of no interest to anyone locally. Or they may be unaware of what outsiders say or think about them.

It can help if local residents know about you and what you do, perhaps taking pride in living in the town where you exist. Or is yours just one of those vague occupants of the trading estate on the fringe of town? If asked your whereabouts by someone visiting you, would they know your location?

- What happens when a store has job vacancies? Every applicant is a possible customer, but the majority of applicants have to be disappointed. How nicely are they thanked for applying?

- What happens when there is an accident involving staff? Does the hospital understand your business and is its staff aware of the health or safety hazards which are peculiar to your business?

- When you have building extension plans before a local authority planning committee, do the butcher and baker councillors understand your business?

- Do career masters or sixth form teachers and head teachers know your business sufficiently well to recommend school leavers to apply for your vacancies? Or do they deter possible applicants with misgivings about you?

- Does the local newspaper or radio station understand you and find you newsworthy, and give you credit for achievement? Or do they only find you interesting when the news is bad? Another strike at Jackson's! ... or congratulations on winning a Queen's Award?

- Is your business recognised as a good employer and a contributor to the good reputation and prosperity of the locality? Do you contribute to the popularity of the town as a place in which to live, work or shop? What part do you play as a business leader in the activities and associations of the town such as the local chamber of commerce, sports clubs, charities or cultural societies?

Some companies have endowed hospital beds, given equipment to technical colleges, sponsored local sports teams, supplied books to libraries, made interest-free loans to societies, put up prizes at local events, supplied floats for carnivals, offered prizes, bursaries and scholarships to schools and colleges, or headed the subscription lists for local charities. They are seen to be responsible members of the community.

A community relations campaign can be an important part of the in-house PR programme, whether you are a High Street shopkeeper or a local manufacturer. Yours may be a large national company with local branch offices or stores or industrial units. How well do you look after ground roots community relations wherever you have locations? This can apply to chains of supermarkets or other stores, banks, insurance companies, building societies and other businesses which have hundreds of local branches as well as to those which have only one location.

Yours can be the sort of business which causes problems like noise, dirt, heavy traffic, fumes or effluent. Because of what you make, such as some chemicals, you may be regarded as dangerous. How well do you control these hazards in the public interest, and how well is this publicly understood? Or understood by public authorities including the police, doctors, hospitals, ambulance and fire services? A good deal of social responsibility is involved. We are all aware of terrible disasters which have occurred, perhaps because insufficient care was taken. We all remember Aberfan, Bhopal, Chernobyl, and numerous river pollutions, nuclear waste radiation escapes, asbestos scares and gas explosions.

If you are BNFL, how do you re-educate the public about your safety and integrity when countries across the other side of the world send nuclear fuel back because you have let someone falsify the relevant records?

We live in a world of great industrial dangers. If yours is that type of business how well do you prepare or protect your community? This is also part of the crisis management discussed in Chapter 20.

Community relations are therefore the very essence of public relations. It really does start on the doorstep, and a good neighbour policy is absolutely essential.

How can you organise an effective community relations programme? Remember, it can not only contribute to good relations with external publics but help to enhance internal relations. Employees will be happiest to work for an employer who is highly regarded locally. It enhances their individual status and helps to make them proud of their jobs. They don't want to work for a firm which is disliked or criticised by their friends, neighbours, customers or other people with whom they come into contact.

The implications of your community relations can be deep-rooted and widespread. They could affect your staff stability or ability to recruit staff.

Let us begin with the media since the media can have a blanket effect and reach a multitude and variety of people in the community, and possibly all or most of the people you need to reach.

Be aware of the kinds of media in the area. They include regional morning, evening and weekly newspapers, not forgetting free sheets and local magazines. Also, be aware of radio and TV programmes covering your area. Make sure that branch managers and works managers are familiar with their local media. This means studying papers and programmes which you may not always read, see or listen to.

Make friends with the media. Respond to them well if they seek interviews. Invite them to call on you. Show them round. Hold open days for journalists and broadcasters. If you do run into trouble, you are likely to get more sympathetic treatment if journalists have already been behind the scenes and know how you operate, and know you personally. Listen to what they have to say. You may be surprised how little they know about your business. Don't assume your business is an open book. Journalists have to deal with hundreds of topics, and sometimes they are new to the job and know nothing about you.

Invite journalists to your events like sports days or Christmas parties. Let them feel welcome. Always have time for them. Send them your house journal, both internal and external. They may like to read your annual report and accounts. Regard them as the focal point of the community. You may not always like what they print, but don't attack them. Tomorrow is always another day, and memories are short. You cannot always be right and they cannot always be wrong.

Your house journal may interest certain people outside the office, shop or factory. Think who should go on the mailing list. The mayor, the chief constable, the matron, the vicar, the secretary of the chamber of commerce, head teachers, the manager of the job centre. Don't forget your pensioners who still live in the local community and talk about their old firm.

Local events provide the opportunity to put your best face forward. You can give prizes at flower shows, athletic meetings, drama and music festivals, agricultural shows, race meetings and tennis tournaments. You could contribute to Christmas lights in the High Street, a float at the annual carnival, a small stand at the village fete, or support the local brass band. Think about the opportunities, and don't wait to be asked. You may even be able to initiate an event, or serve on an organising committee.

Some businesses, especially those with manufacturing plants, are interesting to visit. Local clubs and societies or schools can be encouraged to bring groups for tours. This has already been discussed elsewhere, but it is worth repeating here.

Exhibitions are another way of reaching communal audiences. This may involve participation in public exhibitions which may be mobile, or set up at a local hotel or other venue, or mounted permanently at your premises. An exhibition on your own location may be a reason for inviting party visits, or it may be an additional attraction during visits.

Some exhibitions are big features of community and general public relations. Famous examples are Philips' Evoluon science exhibition at Eindhoven, Lego's children's parks in Denmark and the UK and the ITC Television and Radio Gallery in London. Such exhibitions can tell the story or the history of a company, display its range of products or services, or explain how the product is produced.

A brilliant exhibition, making use of video and sound effects, is that at the Thames Barrier, and another is that on the raising and reconstruction of the Mary Rose at Portsmouth Harbour. Such exhibitions are worth visiting to study the techniques employed.

But private exhibitions do not have to be elaborate or costly. They can be mounted on panels, making good use of photographs and drawings, which can be transportable and erected in public libraries, on station concourses, in foyers of hotels, theatres and other buildings, or taken to careers evenings at schools.

Providing speakers for meetings is another useful community relations activity, but it is important to train such speakers, however articulate they may be. Don't just send along a salesman because he has the gift of the gab. He may bore people with sales talk. Speakers need to be able to interest an audience, perhaps confining their talks to the brevity required for after-lunch speeches, and being able to answer questions. A team of such speakers needs to be developed so that speakers can be offered, or speakers are available when requests are received. Numerous local clubs and societies (not forgetting schools) welcome and seek speakers. These include women's and church groups, chambers of commerce, horticultural societies, youth clubs, sports clubs, professional societies (e.g. publicity clubs, branches of the Institute of Marketing), pensioners' clubs, and organisations like Rotary and Round Table. If you have a local branch of the Association of Speakers Clubs, they can help with training your people and offering opportunity to practice presentations in a friendly atmosphere, before the real thing.

Visual aids such as slides, films or videos (which may already exist for general PR purposes) can be used to augment speakers, or they can be offered on loan for showing by the organisers of local meetings. Film or video evenings can be offered with speaker/operator and projector or playback equipment. For smaller audiences, excellent presentations can be built using a computer program such as Microsoft's Powerpoint, which can then be shown on a laptop or monitor quite adequately for a round-the-table meeting.

There can also be combinations of speaker, portable exhibition and video presentation, and events can be organised on company premises or at a hotel or public hall for invited audiences. These audiences may be groups representing customers, particular publics or potential employees, or members of groups which seek outside visits.

The means of reaching the community, or particularly relevant sections of it, are therefore numerous and varied, and they invite the enthusiasm, ingenuity and organising ability of the in-house PR department. Many people in an organisation can contribute as speakers, guides and hosts. Some of this work will require special or part-time staff, but few companies are without such resources, and there are usually capable employees who enjoy taking on such roles in addition to their normal duties. It can be very rewarding to talk about one's own work, and to enjoy the social side of public events.

19

How Can PR Help Me Export?

'One half of the world does not know how the other half lives.'
English proverb

Do you want to open up overseas markets, or extend the ones you already have?

You can use PR techniques to augment the efforts of salesmen, agents, importers or licensees, or as pathfinder exercises in potential markets. Some of them will cost you nothing beyond your time and cooperation. You can often exploit material you already have such as pictures, feature articles, films or videos.

Unless you have a universally acceptable product like CocaCola or Kodak film, global marketing seldom exists. There are usually regional or national markets. Some products could never be sold in Arab or Chinese markets because they offend those cultures. Others may not suit certain climates. It is therefore necessary, first of all, to identify the markets where sales are possible. For logistical reasons it may also be necessary to determine priority markets. Having done this, the opportunities for using PR can be analysed, and the methods defined.

What do you want to do? Support an existing agency, subsidiary or licensee? Back up your travelling overseas sales force? Or prepare the ground for entry into a new foreign market?

Remember, however well-known your company and its products or services are in your home market, they are less known, probably little known, and maybe unknown in a foreign country. It may be an advantage that you are British, Western, European or foreign, but it could also be a disadvantage. Some countries have protectionist policies to favour indigenous production. Others are politically opposed for a variety of reasons.

Arabs may accuse you of trading with Israel, black Africans may object to your South African association, and Malaysians may adopt a 'Look East' (pro-Japanese) or 'Buy Malaysian' policy.

There are some places where you cannot win. The Europeans are still generally not happy with British meat products The Americans retaliated to the EU ban on American grain by imposing a hefty import duty on gin and cheese.

Before contemplating an export PR programme you need to be certain that you can not only satisfy market demands, but that you will be welcome.

Assuming, then, that you have identified the countries to which you wish to direct a PR programme, a first consideration will be the availability of media by which to convey your messages. The media will differ country by country, and nowhere will you find a replica of the British media situation.

Britain is blessed with a very large and varied press with big circulations and readerships, both nationally and regionally. This is encouraged by the presence of a large, literate population with high living standards living in a compact area with huge centres of population and excellent road, rail and air communications. Even in the industrialised world this is different from Australia, Canada, France, Germany, Japan or the United States. It does not compare with countries, large or small, like India or Singapore.

Thus, you have to start by looking at each country in turn. There may be no national newspapers. A big circulation newspaper may sell no more copies than the The Times or The Independent. There may be several languages in which different newspapers are printed. The trade press may not exist, and there may be few consumer magazines. In a large country, there may be isolated media centres which are hundreds or thousands of miles apart.

These are not insuperable difficulties, but they are differences which call for careful selection of publications, and possibly the necessity to employ expert translators.

You can mail or e-mail news releases, pictures and feature articles direct from the UK. Addresses can be found in the overseas volume of Benn's Media Directory. Overseas mailings and wire services are offered by Universal News Services. If you want first-class translators and distribution of releases and articles by a firm with an international reputation, you can hire the services of EIBIS, who currently hold data on around 38,000 trade and other publications world-wide..

Or you can use the services of the Central Office of Information which distributes stories which are good publicity for Britain. Vital to this sort of news release distribution is the relevance of it to local readers. If the product or service is about an export order, or can be related to overseas needs, or can be demonstrated as satisfying these needs, the story is more likely to be published. The same applies to photographs and feature articles. People in Turkey or Tasmania don't want to read about British applications.

For example, one edition of an international magazine had every article and picture demonstrating the use of the company's products in different countries. Readers could relate to these examples. Even if there was not a story about their particular country, readers could see that the products were of international application, and could apply to them.

Once again we see the need for thoughtfulness in PR, the need to put yourself in other people's shoes. You have to ask yourself what would interest them, repeating the criteria of media relations that your material must be of interest and value to the recipients of your message.

Translations

The quality of translations can make or break export PR when you are dealing in foreign languages. No doubt you have come across some of the comic errors in Dutch bulb catalogues, Japanese camera manuals and other foreign literature. Tulips grow six inches short instead of tall, people are exposed at exhibitions, and (with Indians the world over) posters are postals.

If you are dealing with North America you need an English/American dictionary because correct translations are critical. If you get it wrong they think you are 'quaint' and probably live in or want to sell the Tower of London including the Crown Jewels. Isn't it odd how, for more than sixty years, British people have been watching American films and for fifty years listening to talkies, without noticing that the Americans speak another language and spell and pronounce English words differently? Yet, that's the first thing Americans notice when confronted by British English. They think our spellings and pronunciations are funny, wrong or Olde English. They call a back garden a yard, a lift an elevator, a sweet a candy, a biscuit a cookie, a railway a railroad, a motor-car an automobile, an aeroplane an airplane, a holiday a vacation, an underground railway a subway, a waistcoat a vest, a boot a trunk, and the autumn is known as the fall.

In the PR, advertising and marketing worlds there are totally different sets of jargon which must be very confusing for students in places like Australia, Hong Kong or Singapore who read both American and British textbooks. You may have to ask yourself which 'English' terminology is most familiar to, say, the Japanese. In some fields, compromise has been achieved, as with acceptance in the computer industry of spellings like disk for disc and program for programme.

The point is that once a translation contains a mistake in grammar, spelling or word usage, credibility is lost and the reader suspects that other information is wrong. This may sound silly but it is true. It is difficult to take seriously something which contains an absurd error of translation. Immediately, it becomes a caricature, like a stage or TV comedian taking off a foreigner and producing a giggling audience. Foreigners are always funny.

One English book on PR was reviewed in a Canadian magazine, and the reviewer commented that it was written in quaint English. They air a programme, not broadcast it; piggyback goods on railroad flat wagons but we piggyback questions on omnibus research questionnaires; they call large hoardings billboards but we lean small billboards outside shops; films are, of course, movies in the USA.

This is mentioned at length because it not only concerns export PR to Canada and the USA, but also that addressed to those parts of the world where the locals are confronted by the duality of British-English and American-English. The French have been wise to insist on retaining the purity of their language. The odd thing about the most distinctly different American pronunciations is that they originated from Devonshire, from the old Devonshire sailors who first settled in the American colonies. Maybe that's why Devonshire people sound like Americans.

Correct or appropriate translations apply to every worded message and that includes PR stories, advertisements, labels and packages, stuffers and instruction manuals. The Americans are very bad at shipping goods to Europe with instructions on packages which are irrelevant to European use. This carelessness can be regarded as a superior attitude if not downright insulting. If you are an importer of American goods, it's a point to remember. American snobbery can be offensive.

Finally, here are some important points you should remember about translations. Foreigners may well speak English (and other languages besides their own) but however linguistically skilful they may be, their vocabulary will be limited in those languages they use less frequently. So, keep your vocabulary short and popular, and don't use too much jargon. It can be helpful to use synonyms to clarify meanings, and technical words should be defined for the translator.

External house journals

An example of the use of an external house journal has already been given. The publication of such a magazine for export PR purposes has many advantages, and the cost can be minimised when its reach and influences are assessed.

This kind of private magazine is kept free of domestic internal news and contains feature articles and illustrations of interest to your customers. The readership must be specific for this is not merely a prestige journal to impress people. That would be a waste of time and money. It must be a practical read for people who will benefit from reading it. They could be politicians, agents, buyers, users, dealers and customers according to the nature of the product.

A large part of your trading world will be English-speaking, and it may be possible to print English language copies for distribution to many countries, certainly for Commonwealth countries and other ex-British colonies. But be careful of those countries where people speak and do business in English, but probably read and write very little English. In their case, it would be both courteous and sensible to send them a magazine printed in their language only. This applies throughout Europe.

However, other problems may arise if your journal is to circulate in the Gulf states where the national language is Arabic, but the majority of the population is non-Arabic and may comprise more than a hundred nationalities. Apart from various Arab and European nationalities there will be Indians, Pakistanis, Bangladeshis, Filipinos, Thais, Japanese and scores of others. The solution here (as the Arabs have found) is to adopt English as the second language for everyone. Thus, a house journal for circulation in the Middle East really needs to be in two languages, Arabic and English, if it is to be read by the majority of educated and literate buyers of your products and services.

The external house magazine used internationally enjoys the special advantages that it is mailed direct to identified readers; it is educational and therefore very interesting to its readers; it is a rarity in non-industrialised countries where there is a dearth of magazines. Unlike so much received in industrialised countries, it will not be regarded or discarded as junk mail. Readers will probably receive little mail. Your journal will therefore be welcomed, and it may enjoy a large readership and is likely to be kept for a long time.

You will therefore benefit from taking great care over the production of such journals. They must not be disguised sales literature. They must be legitimate journals that look and read like commercially produced ones, but you must judge the market and decide whether it is to look like The Sun, The Economist or Business. The writing, design, format and printing must be realistic, otherwise credibility will be sacrificed.

Sales tours

A PR build-up for overseas sales trips may help, and this can be done once the itinerary is agreed. The PR department writes a biographical story about the company's representative (especially if he is a senior person or a director), with a statement about the purpose of his visit and this, together with a captioned photograph is sent in advance to newspapers, magazines and, in some cases, news agencies covering each staging post.

A number of overseas newspapers like to report the arrival of interesting visitors, and provided the person is something of a company VIP and not just a salesman doing his rounds, this is PR coverage worth seeking. British Trade International (until May 1999, the British Overseas Trade Board) can be valuable in helping to organise export drives and giving support to Britain's world salesmen. They may be able to set up meetings for you with buyers, arrange for you to give video presentations, and their local press officer or commercial attache may agree to issue a news release on your visit.

For instance, British High Commissions in some countries issue daily news bulletins, circulating them to the media and to public places such as hotels.

Such introductory publicity is not without its risks, although the following true story is probably the exception to prove the rule.

The technical director of a certain British company was touring the Caribbean and the company PRO preceded his calls by sending local editors a picture story about his impending arrival at each island. This director was not amused to arrive in Trinidad and to be shown a newspaper report on his arrival, illustrated with a picture of a black man with the director's name printed below it. It transpired that the black man had been arrested for murder and the wrong picture had been pasted down for each story. This, of course, meant that the director's picture illustrated the murder story!

Use of video

The video documentary has been mentioned many times in this book. Better than clumsy 16mm or 8mm film, and so much easier to use, the VHS video is the boon of modern PR. Its uses are so many that its cost must be recovered many times. Export PR is where video can be a tremendous asset.

World-wide distribution is possible through the Central Office of Information who acquire films and videos, catalogue them and offer them abroad. They must be free of advertising and not be blown-up commercials. Major outlets for them are overseas television stations which are greedy for free programmes. Provided your video will interest a large popular audience, it will be used.

The film can also be borrowed by people abroad who order through the British High Commission or embassy, and the film or video is flown out from London.

Videos are easily carried by company representatives when they go abroad, and they can be shown at sales meetings, press receptions, during talks and on exhibition stands. Beforehand, you should check that your video is compatible with local hardware for playing it.

On-the-spot service

To use local sales agents to distribute press material may be dangerous as they may misunderstand the nature of PR, confuse it with advertising, and approach the wrong people at media offices. Best, therefore, to control distribution yourself unless you can appoint a reliable PR consultant.

If you are dealing with the main trading centres of the world, there are PR consultancies with international networks of offices. Addresses of PR consultancies world-wide will be found in the Hollis Press and Public Relations Annual.

Trade fairs, British weeks and export information

British Trade International promotes British exhibitions, British Weeks and British Pavilions and trade fairs, in which you may care to participate. British Trade International is a global network dedicated to helping UK business compete successfully throughout the world – they publish a great deal of information about foreign markets. In connection with overseas exhibitions and events the BTI also organises publicity and media coverage in the countries concerned. To encourage smaller firms to exhibit abroad, the BTI also offers financial help.

If you are planning an export programme it is well worth contacting the Publicity Unit at 1 Victoria Street, London, SW1H OET for information and advice or visiting their web site at www.dti.gov.uk/ots/. As a taxpayer, you are entitled to all the help you can get from government bodies like the BTI and the COI.

A number of banks offer export information, a digest of international information or regular bulletins on individual countries, and their customers may put their names on the mailing list for regular publications. What has your bank to offer?

The Economist Intelligence Unit publishes numerous overseas reports which are advertised weekly in The Economist. There are also a number of data banks which hold international information, such as Databank Ltd, Harvest and many others.

Your potential overseas markets may be thousands of miles away but a wealth of information and excellent services exist in London. If you are an enterprising exporter, you will have no difficulty in planning and executing an effective export PR programme from your home base in the UK. Many of these services will be found among the useful addresses in the Appendices.

20

How Do I Use PR in a Crisis?

'Crisis! Crisis! What crisis?'

James Callaghan

Has your business ever suffered a crisis? If so, what did you do, how did you deal with the media, how did you come out of it? Or perhaps you've been lucky and you've never experienced a disaster situation. Maybe, you think it will never happen to you !

Nothing is certain in this modern world where we are so often at the mercy of events, people and technologies over which we have absolutely no control.

Crisis management, and its PR implications, is now a special and rapidly developing area of PR. Some PR consultancies specialise in advising on crisis management: in many well-known PR departments, crisis PR has become a vital function.

It is not only a question of what to do when a crisis blows up but how do you identify likely and unlikely crises, how do you prepare for such a bad day, and what do you do if it happens? It may never happen. Schools have fire drills but not many school fires occur while the pupils are in class.

There are certain crises which could hit any business such as fire, accident, strike, financial loss, scandal or take-over bid. Product failures are not uncommon. You may find that a hacker or a malevolent virus has chopped up your essential data records and has destroyed your hard drive.

External influences could provoke a crisis such as inability to obtain raw materials or components because of a dock strike, winter freeze-up, power failure, or a strike at a supplier's plant. It has happened in a number of industries where there is a great reliance on supplies of vital components, such as in car manufacturing. A scandal could write millions off your share price. It happened to a highly respected and successful company like Guinness, whose shares lost £300m in stock market value between announcement of the DTI investigation and the dismissal of the chairman. And that was only the beginning!

You may be in the holiday, travel or transportation business. Look at the problems Thomson Holidays, P & O Cruises, British Airways and the Grand Hotel, Brighton had, through no fault of their own.

Food manufacturers have had their problems ranging from poisonings to court cases. John West tinned salmon, Farleys baby foods and Perrier all suffered major catastrophes, and odd things have been found in biscuits, chocolates and meat pies. The recall of John West canned salmon cost £2m, and Farleys went bankrupt and were disposed of. A number of hotels and restaurants have had their reputations smirched as a result of prosecutions because kitchens were unhygienic. In some cases, the disaster was unavoidable, but this is not always so.

An initial stage in crisis management is therefore prevention. The PR implications of this should be obvious. If every effort is made to prevent crises happening, the bad PR effects of crises can be avoided. Does that sound too simple?

How often do you have plan B all set up to put into operation if plan A fails? Or do you assume that plan A will always work? In case of transport strikes or weather hazards, newspapers have alternative transport. A large organisation which travels a party of 120 journalists every year to a national event always books coaches as well as train reservations in case there is a rail strike. Only once has it had to fall back on emergency road services – but they were there!

A fail-safe system of organising back-up may be the way to avoid that disaster which only has to happen once to be a disaster. Trying to be clever before the event is not always easy, especially if you are rather proud of an apparently efficient organisation.

Prevention as well as preparation may be combined if you make a really serious attempt to identify both likely and unlikely crises. This means that you quite bluntly admit that you may not be perfect and that the unthinkable just might happen to you. That surrender of pride might save lives, jobs, fortunes and certainly reputation.

Many terrible disasters in recent years have happened because responsible people did not believe they could happen, but they did. The bosses at Barings Bank would not have thought they were vulnerable and so they were not aware until the last minute that Nick Leeson was sucking them dry to the point when they died. Air France did not expect one of their Concordes to crash just outside Paris in July 2000, but it did.

Right now, before you finish reading this book, take a sheet of paper and draw a vertical line down the middle. At the top of the left-hand column write LIKELY, and at the top of the right-hand column write UNLIKELY. Then spend the next hour filling up the two columns. You may have a shock. You will probably sleep badly tonight.

Let's take an imaginary example, say, a manufacturing company which is a pretty broad example covering many products and industries.

Likely

Strike
Explosion
Effluent problem
Pollution problem
Strike at suppliers'
Transportation strike
Faulty production –
   product recall
Competition – lower prices,
   better products, alternative
   product
Government regulations,
   restrictions
Tax changes, e.g. VAT, profits
Loss of major export market
   (e.g. Argentina, Iran, Nigeria)
Fall in share price

Unlikely

Fire
Sabotage – e.g. bombing by
   terrorists, or by pressure group
Riot damage
Earthquake
Company leader held as hostage or
   hi-jacked
Assassination of company leader
Embarrassing investigation by
   newspaper or TV programme
Investigation by government
   commission or committee, e.g.
   Competition Commission, DTI, OFT
Scandal resulting from behaviour
   of company leader
Factory/premises destroyed by
   some outside influence, e.g.

Take-over bid
Increase in a cost, e.g. raw
  material
Collapse of advertising due to
  newspaper or TV strike
Change of government
War, civil war, revolution
Excessive imports, dumping
Death of company leader,
  natural or accidental
Loss of major contract or market
Boycott by group of buyers
Computer systems destroyed or
  disrupted by virus

crashing aircraft, storm, flood
Industrial espionage: theft of
  plans, designs, secret recipes,
  computer records
Costly prototype destroyed
Rival beats you to market with
  identical product
Your activities, services, product
  made illegal
Your product proved to be worthless
  by independent investigators
Consumerist or other pressure group
  oblige you to make changes, e.g.
  use different packaging
Product causing unexpected health
  hazard or side effects (e.g.
  pharmaceuticals)

How near to these lists did you get with yours? Now, ask others in your organisation to prepare their lists. Ask your works manager, personnel manager, safety officer, marketing manager, export manager and whoever handles your PR. Then combine all the non-duplicated items. By this time you may need a very stiff drink to restore your sense of balance!

Your search for possible disasters may be encouraged by the fact that all those listed under Likely and Unlikely in this chapter have happened to some British business somewhere.

Some companies have experienced two or three of these crises, and in every case, management was totally unprepared. They had to get out from under as hard as they could. One company suffered five of those disasters, but fortunately it had a managing director who was a good communicator and who acted quickly to minimise the damage. There may be a very indefinite borderline between 'likely' and 'unlikely'. After all, a medicinal product is marketed because its makers believe it to be efficacious, and yet harmful or viciously dangerous side-effects may not be detected until it has been on the market for some time. So high are the costs of development research that there is great temptation to market a pharmaceutical product in order to recover research costs. A number of famous pharmaceutical companies have caused and paid.the penalty for tragedies, but it may be extremely difficult to decide when adequate research has been conducted and a product is safe to put on the market. The thalidomide tragedy remains to haunt the pharmaceutical industry, and more recently, major problems with breast implants have caused wide legal and economic ripples.

When you have identified potential risks, and wherever possible introduced safeguards, you should set up a permanent crisis management team. Don't make it too big. Four or five members should be enough – people like yourself, your PRO or PR consultant, works manager, safety officer and personnel manager. A small team can maintain easy contact and virtually speak with one voice when trouble breaks.

The team should meet regularly, review any changes or new risks, rehearse action to be taken in the event of a crisis, and be ready to go into action at any time. It is wise to have deputies for each member of the team because members of the team could be sick, away on business or on holiday when desperately needed. Again, a fall-back situation is envisaged.

You should also make sure that communication is always possible between members of the crisis management team. Do they have telephones, radio phones, car radios, necessary vehicles (which might even include a helicopter!) or any other form of communication peculiar to the nature of the industry? Do they also have any necessary protective clothing?

One of the best ways to plan how to deal with emergencies is to be utterly pessimistic. Think of everything that could go wrong, even with your emergency plan. Have you a Plan C? So now list all the things that could go wrong. For starters, here's a list of possibilities:

Things that could go wrong

Telephone out of order	Lights failure
Lack of petrol	Accident to member of team
Roads blocked	Bad weather
Police restrictions	False stories in the media
Computer down	

The biggest problem from a PR point of view is that whatever has gone wrong is bound to be sufficiently dramatic to attract the media. Press, radio and TV journalists will descend upon the scene with ghoulish glee. Bad news is good news, remember. News is what someone, somewhere doesn't want you to print.

Like Barkis, you've got to be willing! And ready and willing.

The crisis team will have been set up to deal with an emergency, and priorities could be saving life, hospitalising people, and assisting the police and fire brigade, but another priority is dealing with the media.

First of all, members of the team must all know and tell the same story, and know how much (for security, legal or personal reasons) they may reveal. The sooner they can tell the most complete story the better. But if there are good reasons for withholding information this must be explained. Some reasons may be:

1   In the event of deaths, next of kin need to be informed first.
2   In the case of insurance claims or legal action, it is usually necessary not to admit any sort of liability otherwise insurers will refuse to indemnify you.
3   For security reasons – because of the nature of contracts, processes and trade secrets, or knock-on or side-effects of the disaster – it may be necessary to be 'economical with the truth'.

Supposing, for instance, there was an unproven risk of contamination. To reveal this to the media might cause a panic, however indignantly journalists might clamour for the right to reveal the facts. They have no rights, only their jobs of making more money for their bosses.

You cannot permit them to profit by your calamity which may involve innocent people who are your concern, and rarely of any genuine concern to the media. The media are not limited to the gutter press, and today they include international news agencies and international satellite TV news services.

You are the host and the teller of tales. You are not the accused being cross-examined by the prosecution. Remember that and keep your nerve. That is important because you have got to recognise the peculiar nature of the media, and work with it to your advantage and not theirs. In a storm the captain does not permit passengers to come on the bridge and tell him how to steer the ship.

Have you ever thought of a crisis situation being like this? Had you regarded it with trepidation as an unpleasant experience in which you are the victim of prying, insistent, won't-take-no-for-an-answer reporters? Of course, they can be a nuisance. They can have a terrier-like persistence. In one example where the company in trouble had three locations, reporters telephoned each in turn, hoping to get a contradictory story from one of them.

But it's a game two can play once you understand them. You can be like certain outspoken members of the Royal Family and say 'Sod off' which in itself gives the media a nice spin to the story. Or you can be thoroughly organised to receive journalists, photographers and cameramen. This is all part of crisis PR planning. Know now how you will deal with the press if anything calamitous happens. Don't wait until they are yammering at the door.

Don't forget that it is your story, your information, your property, your calamity. You don't have to tell anyone anything except those to whom you are responsible, such as your shareholders, your customers, your lawyer, your insurance broker or your banker. Maybe the media can also convey information to these people too, but you have no control over what they will say. Much of the time you will be feeding idle curiosity and entertaining readers and audiences.

This is not being cynical: if the average person did not want to be entertained by dramatic events, Shakespeare's plays (mostly violent) would not have survived, Stephen King's books would not sell by the million to every class of reader, The Sun would not sell four million copies daily, and EastEnders would not have an audience exceeding twelve million. Nowadays almost everybody is an old lady knitting at the foot of the guillotine.

Once, a colleague who was an in-house PRO, was having dinner in an hotel a long way away from base, when the head waiter called him to the telephone. On the line was his managing director, and he was frantic. Apparently some of the company's men had set fire to a client's roof with a blow-lamp. 'The police are here! The fire brigade are here! The press are here! What do I do?' wailed this man. 'Nothing', the PRO told him, 'It's too late', and went back to finish his dinner. If you're the CEO, you can't expect someone five hundred miles away to wave a magic wand and pretend it's never happened.

An almost identical situation happened at a factory which burned down. The police called the MD who arrived, assessed the damage, checked to see if anyone had been hurt, and then walked over to the group of reporters standing at the gate. Briefly, he explained the situation, estimated the value of the possible damage, and confirmed that there had been no casualties. The reporters thanked him and went. The story made a small paragraph in a few papers.

So much depends on the ability of the responsible man or woman on the spot to deal with the media promptly, frankly and simply.

In the case of major disasters which are certain to attract a large number of media representatives, you should be ready with facilities to satisfy them. A briefing room will be essential. Have you such a place that can be put into operation immediately? Has it got, or can it be fitted out with, tables, chairs, telephones? E-mail? What about car-parking? Food? Drinks? Protective clothing such as helmets, goggles, wellies?

Made to feel welcome and their needs looked after, a news-hungry cohort of journalists can be turned into your guests. This may take some stomaching, and one hears some sickening stories about the way journalists have behaved at British airports following air crashes, but much depends on how you plan and rehearse in order to keep control. After all, if you do have to cope with an awkward cuss of a journalist who wants to go it alone you can always throw him out, and the 'sod off' story in the tabloid is not likely to do you any harm.

Bear in mind the acceptable amount of intrusion by the media that their own regulations seemingly apply – do not let yourself become the victim of bullying or coercion by reporters.

So, here you are, holding both ends of the tug-of-war rope and keeping your cool. Not easy, but not impossible. Your first duty is to sort out things at your end and overcome the disaster situation. At the same time you have to carry the media with you, telling them as much as possible.

Later, when the problem has been righted you have the supreme opportunity of gaining some good PR, especially if from the onset and in the meantime the media have recognised that you have played fair with them.

Now you have the opportunity of inviting them to come and see or hear what you have done. Now you can take them on a tour of the once stricken plant, or whatever was the disaster situation, and show them how you have recovered. There is no reason why – if you deserve it – you cannot turn disaster into success.

Bear in mind that you may be vulnerable, after a disaster (which may be more of a disaster in some people's eyes than in others') to attack via the internet. Disaffected customers may set up a hostile web site and broadcast their discontent widely, encouraging others to join in or boycott your company's products or services. Major companies such as Microsoft and McDonalds have suffered at the hands of unhappy customers with their anti-sites. Strong action need to be taken to restore public confidence and company morale.

Product recall

So far we have concentrated on events, but the recall of faulty products also needs to have its rehearsal drill because it can be a dangerous situation which has to be handled urgently. You may think your reputation will suffer if you publicly admit that your product is faulty. This is not so. Customers tend to appreciate your honesty. On the other hand, several European motor-car companies have suffered disfavour because they resisted claims about a fault. Eventually, due to pressure, one of them had to recall the criticised model for modifications.

The costliest recalls are those where stocks have to be retrieved from shops, and the most difficult can be when customers are asked to return products for modification. The first are usually FMCGs stocked by supermarkets and other stores, and the second are usually appliances of which coffee jugs, hair dryers and lawnmowers have been examples. The trouble with the latter is that they may no longer be in the possession of the original buyer.

Because there is usually some danger involved, product recall has to be done boldly, using the right media prominently, enlisting the display services of retailers, and using media relations to have statements published and broadcast.

Watch the press and you may be surprised at the number of product recalls that are made. The urgency and frankness with which they are handled can often be to the credit of the company concerned. When something goes wrong, you may fear that this will discredit your company or product. If the unfortunate situation is handled well it is more likely that customers will appreciate your honesty and helpfulness. The following Hygena announcement is a nice example:

SAFETY WARNING

To all owners of a Hygena Integrated Refrigerator HYG000

It has become apparent that a very small number of the above refrigerators (NOT THE FREEZERS) sold between November 19xx and December 19xx may contain a component which does not meet Hygena's exacting quality standards, and is susceptible to an ageing defect which can in certain circumstances give risk to an electrical failure.

Hygena's commitment to the quality and safety of its merchandise is total and all customers who own a Hygena Integrated Refrigerator HYG000 are asked to ring the following FREEPHONE Telephone Number:

0800-xxx-xxx (between 9am and 6pm any weekday).

Please give your full Name, Address and Telephone Number.

Arrangements will then be made to send to your house a fully qualified engineer who will carry out a full safety check and modification (if necessary) of your appliance, FREE OF CHARGE.

WE APOLOGISE FOR ANY INCONVENIENCE THIS MAY CAUSE

Check back to chapter 6 and the ideas there for dealing with crisis using your web site as an aid. In such circumstances, you need every available resource.

One final word of advice. If the situation or event lends itself to this, make a pictorial record in photographs, slides or video of what went wrong and how you handled it. This will be valuable so that you can take precautions in the future and train people by demonstrating what happened and what you did in a real disaster situation.

21

Why Do I Need to Use Research?

'When an opinion is general, it is usually correct.'
Jane Austen

As a business person, you are probably familiar with marketing research. Your marketing manager will apply research at every step of the game. Since marketing is about producing and selling at a profit what people are likely to buy, their wishes and preferences have to be researched. So does the brand naming, packaging and pricing. Before launching a new product it may be sensible insurance to test market it together with the proposed marketing strategy.

- Your advertising people will also recommend research to discover buying motives, test various copy appeals and commercials, and measure response.
- Media buying will be based on readership and audience surveys.
- Consumer panels will be used to test who buys what, when and how.
- Dealer audit surveys will report on brand shares at point-of-sale.

The above is a very brief sketch of the wealth of research that is applied to marketing and advertising. No doubt you know all about this.

But what about research in PR? If you have an in-house PR department or employ a PR consultant, how much do you spend on research?

You wouldn't be the only person in business who admitted to never spending anything, or even to think about doing so.

To be fair, several of the larger PR consultancies do recommend research to their clients. Some large companies do expect their in-house PR units to apply research. It is in the textbooks, even questioned in PR exams. The trouble is that there are still people who believe that PR is intangible, that you pays your money and takes your chance.

If you spend money on PR, and believe that, you might as well donate your PR budget to a charity. Throughout this book, we have tried to show how PR can benefit your business. Benefits are results. The next chapter deals with results. In PR, research can be used in two ways.

- First, it can be used to reveal the current situation so that PR methods can be applied to solve communication problems.

- Second, it can be used to test the extent to which the PR programme is succeeding (or failing!) to solve these problems. In this, research can also be used to test the effectiveness of the methods used.

We may use primary (original) research or secondary (existing) research. Primary research can consist of surveys and other studies. Secondary research can make use of published data. Some studies may consist of observation and experience, and not require surveys. Thus a great number of research methods can be applied, some of which are simple and inexpensive.

You will doubtless agree that there is really no point in spending money on PR unless it achieves something. But what? A collection of press cuttings may please your vanity, but what did this coverage achieve? You may be proud of sponsoring something, but where did it get you? Cost effectiveness applies to PR as well as to everything else you spend money on. Or had this not occurred to you? Are you still bemused by the favourable this or that syndrome which is often associated with PR?

The simple logic is this: if a PR programme has specific objectives there must be results, good, bad or indifferent. If this logic is pursued, research of one kind or another is involved from start to finish. If it is not, how do you know how to start and what was the finish? Even a horse-race punter uses some kind of research – studying form – but PR is not a gamble.

Or do you think it is? Is that why you have not used PR in your business, or why you use it ineffectively? Do you just budget so much for PR and expect someone to get on with it? Do you have a contract with a PR consultancy with no allocation for research? Many business people do, and they are often contemptuous about PR. No wonder!

Would you fly in an aircraft unless you believed it was airworthy, that it had a qualified pilot, and that it was normal for the aircraft to arrive at its destination? PR should be exactly like that.

Before planning a PR programme, the first step should be to assess the situation. That means finding out what the perceived current image is, what your publics know or think about your organisation, your products or your services. What are their attitudes, their misconceptions? What is the extent of their hostility, prejudice, apathy or ignorance?

You cannot assume that you know the answers, and so it is necessary to appreciate the situation. You can engage a research unit to conduct a communication audit (internally as well as externally), an opinion poll or an image study. You will be familiar with the concept of opinion polls.

Image studies set out to compare attitudes towards your organisation and your rivals over a number of issues.

The kind of research may depend on your type of business. It may be important to test the attitudes of your distributors, shareholders, the City, customers, or opinion leaders.

These investigations will reveal where your communication problems lie, and PR is about problem solving. Once you are fully aware of the situation – and it could be surprisingly different from what you assumed it was – you can draw up your list of objectives. These objectives will be what you want PR to do for you – change your image because you have changed your business, improve your dealer relations, help your export programme, make the City aware of your financial strengths, educate the market about your product and service and so on. These have been the themes of previous chapters. But now we are bringing them together in a coherent overall plan because they spring from initial research into your situation in all these areas.

Next, who are your publics? With whom must you communicate in order to achieve these objectives? Again, another long list will be developed. It will be very different from the clear-cut target audiences (e.g. sex, age, income and social grades or market segments) to which you address your advertising. This is not advertising: PR is very different from advertising because you are now dealing with numerous sub-groups of people. You are not dealing with the general public, that mythical mass of undefined people.

How do you reach these publics? Can you use existing media like the press, radio and TV, or do you need to create media like house journals, documentary videos or private exhibitions? The media can be researched, and cost benefit analyses made to compare their likely effectiveness.

All this must be costed, and it is a question of whether you budget what it will cost to achieve your objectives, or you start with a budget which exercises constraints upon how many objectives you can afford to try to achieve.

Finally comes the assessment of results. This planning sequence can be set out in the shape of the following six-point PR planning formula:

1. appreciation of the situation
2. definition of objectives
3. definition of publics
4. choice of media and techniques
5. budget
6. assessment of results.

Any PR department or PR consultancy should base its proposals for the next financial year on this sort of plan. But you cannot do one without the other. It begins with appreciation of the situation. There are three ways of arriving at this appreciation:

- You can *guess.*

- You can *assume* (and a lot of PROs and PR consultancies do base proposals on the assumptions presented to them by the management of their companies or clients. These assumptions are almost bound to be false).

- You can *conduct research* to find out what the situation actually is.

This chapter will be confined to research which should be conducted at the planning stage. The next chapter will deal with methods of assessing results.

If you want to test awareness, knowledge or attitudes, you can use an opinion poll. The questionnaire will ask questions which seek a Yes, No or Don't Know response. The questionnaire can also be varied to include lists and respondents will be asked to state which items they know or use.

For example, one manager wanted to know how many people of a certain kind had heard of his company. The name of the company was placed in a list of the other leading companies carrying out similar business. Now, it was impossible for him to know the answer, although he could assume that because his was a multi-million pound concern, it should be very well-known. He was amazed by the result. Only two percent of the sample had heard of his company, whereas sixty percent had heard of his biggest rival.

Immediately, a major communication problem was revealed. It could not be solved by advertising, but it was solved by PR.

This example can be repeated in the cases of totally different types of organisations. Three typical ones concern an insurance company, a university and an advertising agency.

Opinion polls have been conducted in Britain for more than fifty years by Social Surveys (Gallup Poll) Ltd, and if you follow the political polls you will be aware of many other firms such as MORI, NOP and Harris. Opinion polls are by no means limited to political forecasts and Gallup, for instance, apply sophisticated technology to producing music charts based on a weekly analysis of sales of CDs and cassettes, using overnight data retrieval systems at 500 shops. The image study is another form of research, and this is particularly useful in the case of an industrial company where the sample can consist of a cross-section of typical buyers who may buy materials or components from a number of suppliers.

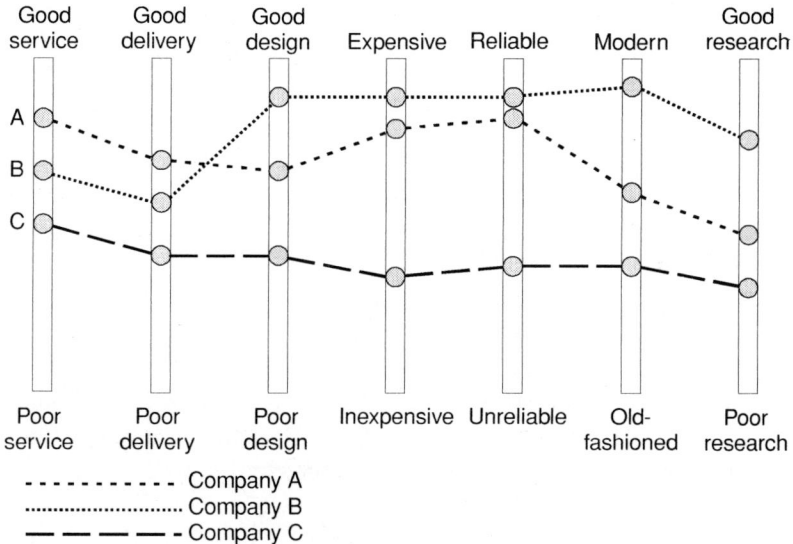

Example of an Image Study presented graphically.
More than three companies can, of course be compared.
(Based on a chart in 'Effective PR Planning' by Frank Jefkins)

The questionnaire names all the suppliers of which one is your company. A series of questions is asked on relevant topics such as price, service, delivery, research and so on so that it is possible to compare (in graphical form) the opinions held about each supplier.

Thus an image is created of each company, and you can compare the perceived image of your company against those of your rivals. This revelation of strengths and weaknesses can indicate how your PR effort should be directed. It may be that your buyers have the wrong image because you have failed to communicate effectively in the past.

For example, a foreign multi-national may possess a very unpatriotic image, and be thought to be a drag on the economy when in fact it's contributing immensely to the economy through employment, taxes and exports.

Another might be considered old-fashioned in its production methods when in fact it is highly computerised and automated.

Yet another might be criticised for poor research and development when it actually has one of the world's finest laboratories.

These misconceptions are not known until they are revealed through some sort of survey or analysis, and they lead to PR programmes to overcome those negative states of hostility, prejudice and ignorance. This is where the information and educational aspects of PR come to the fore. They are different from advertising. They are more specific than trying to create favourable images and favourable climates of opinion. They are about people knowing facts. They are about producing change, about correcting false ideas.

In the above examples we have discussed specially initiated research. However, it is possible that some of the research already conducted for marketing and advertising purposes possesses information which can be used for PR purposes. These opportunities should not be overlooked, and PR personnel should be given access to all such existing reports.

Another way of reducing or eliminating the cost of special PR research is for the PR personnel to co-operate with the marketing department and have PR-type questions incorporated in various marketing surveys.

Some research can be relatively simple. A foreign bank once asked how it was regarded in the City. Six reliable sources were asked what they knew or thought about this bank. Without exception, they said they wouldn't touch it with a barge pole. The last respondent was asked why the researcher was getting this thumbs down response. The answer was simple: the bank had omitted to place an entry in the largest directory of world banks and was therefore considered to be disreputable. Each of the sources had been checking this directory.

Sometimes an inexpensive postal or telephone survey can reveal valuable information. For instance, what do readers think of your house journal? Do you ever ask them? One consultant was sceptical about the value of a client's external house journal, of which he was immensely proud. He agreed to the despatch of a brief questionnaire to all his readers. Not one replied, which was answer enough. The shocked client abandoned his useless publication.

This was more diplomatic than telling the client that his customers must have been bored by all the pictures and stories about himself. Vanity publications can be very bad PR.

You may have to choose between various publications, radio or TV programmes to which you would like to offer exclusive feature articles or, in the cases of broadcast media, material or facilities for programmes, e.g. interviews, videos or visits.

How do you evaluate them? Research can take two forms. You can study published data such as audited circulation figures (ABC), readership figures (JICNARS), radio audience figures (JICRAR), or TV audience figures-including weekly charts (BARB). You may decide it is better if your article appears in The Director rather than Business, or that you are interviewed by Terry Wogan rather than Jonathan Dimbleby. The analysis can look at figures and kinds of readership or audience.

But supposing you need to create media in order to reach specific publics. What will you spend your money on? What is likely to be most cost-effective, even perhaps for the same money? You may think videos are old-hat, or that no-one bothers to read external house journals. Well, that's only your opinion or hunch. It's a pretty risky and unjustified value judgement. Why not apply cost benefit analysis?

The following is a fictitious example, but it is the sort of test you could apply – or ask your PR people to apply – before taking a decision. The plus or minus figures will depend on your business and how you would employ the three media, but in the example the versatility and flexibility of video is brought out. The exercise does invite you to evaluate a variety of media against a set of critical values. It can reveal strengths and weaknesses of different media as they apply to you and your needs.

PLUS FACTOR METHOD OF EVALUATING MEDIA

	Private exhibition	Video cassette	External house journal
1. Ease of production	6	8	10
2. Size of audience	8	6	10
3. Movement	8	10	0
4. Sound	10	10	0
5. Colour	10	10	10
6. Ease of updating	7	8	10
7. Ease of operation	5	10	10
8. Impact	10	8	6
9. Impression created	10	8	6
	74	**78**	**62**

Without such a test, you could have blundered into a disappointing choice. This is not to say that the test is conclusive. Obviously it all depends on the quality of the private exhibition, video cassette or external house journal.

There are also other controlling factors such as whether you have a vehicle for the travelling exhibition, already have a video studio, and already have a house journal editor. These could affect the first valuation, ease of production or the seventh one, ease of operation.

Further examples of the use of research in PR will be discussed in the next chapter on evaluating results.

22

How Do I Evaluate PR Results?

'This is not the end. It is not even the beginning of the end.
But it is, perhaps, the end of the beginning.'
Sir Winston Churchill
Mansion House, November 10, 1942
on the Battle of Egypt

Now we come to the proof of the pudding. If PR is to be tangible and cost-effective, and if you have set out to achieve specific objectives, you should be able to evaluate the results of all your PR efforts. How can this be done?

There are three ways of assessing results, and they will depend on the objectives you have set and the methods you have used including the kind of media you have chosen.

- The first method is **experience.** What changes have affected the situation which was assessed before planning the PR campaign?

- The second method is **observation.** Some changes will be physically apparent or visible.

- The third method is **scientific** or by means of various tests, calculations, and use of research studies.

Some of these methods will cost no more than the time to carry out the assessment. Independent research will obviously cost a research fee, but in many cases (e.g. an opinion poll) it will repeat the initial research to measure the extent or nature of the change of opinion, awareness, knowledge or reversal of misconceptions which has been achieved.

Experience

If your problem was complaints from customers, including distributors, perhaps because of misuse of the product, misunderstanding of instructions, or even a defective product requiring a recall operation, the situation could now be very different. Assuming the complaints had been dealt with satisfactorily, or the reason removed – if educational PR or a rewritten instruction manual had improved enjoyment of the product or if the recall had been handled well – the results could be reduction in complaints, but an increase in recommendations and praise or satisfied customers. Feedback from your salesmen, distributors or customers can provide the experience.

You may experience other changes such as more replies to your vacancy advertisements, or more appropriate ones from applicants with a better understanding of your business. This could save your personnel department expense in placing vacancy advertisements, or time in having to deal with irrelevant applications.

If there had been sales resistance from distributors, which your PR campaign had aimed to overcome, your sales force should now experience a better welcome and response from the trade. This will be fed back in salesmen's reports. The prejudice of buyers may have been a problem (e.g. local authorities accepting a commercial service which they had resisted before, payers of regular bills being willing to pay by direct debit, or household insurance policy holders being willing to insure adequately).

You may find that the visitors to your web site stay longer and are more interested in buying your goods or services. If your site is more informative than previously, then the quality and quantity of hits is likely to improve as people understand your business and philosophy better. Careful web design is essential if you wish to capture people's imagination as well as their wallets.

These are just a few examples. It depends what your communication problems were, what you wanted out of PR, and how you went about using PR techniques to achieve your ends. Perhaps even at this late stage – when you think about the results that are possible – you will recognise fresh opportunities for making good use of PR. There is no magic about PR, but in practical terms it can be very much your business.

Observation

This may be similar to experience, but there can be results which can actually be seen to happen.

Internally, are safety precautions better observed, such as wearing protective helmets or goggles? The steel industry made a special film on this subject which was shown to employees. Are vehicles kept cleaner? Is there greater punctuality or less absenteeism? Are there fewer road accidents among your drivers?

Externally, do dealers use your display material more effectively, perhaps as the result of regular trade press stories and pictures; do passengers use your road systems, airports or railway stations more efficiently, perhaps as a result of radio announcements; and has your store traffic improved because more customers are aware of your range of merchandise or special customer services such as car-parking, thanks to coverage in the local press?

As with experience, a detailed analysis of the hits recorded on your web site will give you a clear view of the types of visitors and the times they stayed. Obviously, if the prime purpose of your site is to keep customers informed and enthusiastic, and your PR efforts are aimed at increasing awareness of their needs through careful listening to their stories, then the business that your site creates will increase.

For more information on web site design and management, read 'Secrets of E-commerce' by Laurel Alexander, Management Books 2000, 2000.

Tests, calculations and research

Now we come to systematic studies of data. Some of that, like media coverage, provides a form of desk research because you possess press cuttings and monitored broadcasts supplied by agencies or collected yourself.

A good example occurs with sponsorships where specialist agencies supply records of press, radio and TV coverage, not only by volume but by publication, radio and TV programme and station, often with dates. An event like the London Marathon is recorded in great detail.

There are two elementary ways of evaluating media coverage, one good and one bad. A tally can be made of the volume of press coverage in terms of column inches or centimetres, while the volume of radio and TV coverage can be counted in hours or minutes. That makes an interesting and useful record.

However, some people make the false calculation of multiplying volume by the value as if the space or time had been bought at advertising rates.

Well, what do you think about equating coverage with the equivalent advertising cost? Do you like to make that sort of evaluation? Do you like to say, 'Look how much free advertising we got!'?

You may find this hard to swallow because those monetary figures give you something concrete to go on, and you are trying to put some tangible evaluation on press cuttings and broadcasts.

A motor-car manufacturer boasted of the thousands of pounds of free advertising he had obtained by giving away a car on a TV show. There was uproar in TV circles, and the producer of the programme got fired!

Rate card evaluations of media coverage are nonsense when you think about them seriously. You would never normally have bought that space or time on those dates in those publications or programmes. Moreover, we are talking about editorial space and programme time, which is priceless. Until such time as sponsored broadcasting is more widely sanctioned in the UK, you cannot easily buy programme time.

If you sponsored something like a snooker championship or golf tournament, it would be screened for hours with frequent reference to your company. To buy that time would cost a king's ransom, and to evaluate the coverage in advertising terms would be utterly unrealistic. Therefore, it's no yardstick at all.

So let's forget this mythical form of evaluation and let's examine how much more precisely a genuine assessment can be made.

What is the quality of the coverage? In the USA, this sort of research has been computerised so that all sorts of qualities such as medium, volume, position, date and tone of comment have been given values to achieve a reading so that comparison can be made.

One way of calculating quality is to apply JICNARS readership, JICRAR radio audience, and BARB television audience figures to the coverage so that figures can be produced showing that so many thousand or million people of specified demographic types had opportunities to see (OTS) or hear publications or broadcasts.

This can also be demonstrated if we consider something peculiar to Britain: the broad class breakdown of the national dailies, using the A, B, C^1, C^2, D, E social grades adopted by JICNARS. It was set out more fully in Chapter 5.

The Times	]	A
Financial Times	]	
Daily Telegraph	]	
The Guardian	]	B
The Independent	]	
Daily Express	]	C^1
Daily Mail	]	
The Sun	]	
Daily Mirror	]	C^2, D
The Star	]	

This is very broad because obviously there are people who do read more than one class of newspaper but it is a breakdown much used in planning advertising media schedules. It also applies to PR because there are few PR news releases which justify a blanket mailing to the national press. However, it is not always possible to control publication, and newspapers may receive stories from news agencies, or initiate stories themselves. For example, an insider scandal story may be reported by all the media yet a normal financial PR story would have a more selective distribution.

Similarly, there can be social and economic breakdowns of more specialised publications, ranging from the women's press to computer journals. Coverage in some may be gratifying but wasteful in others. Therefore, another form of evaluation is the Media Coverage Rating Chart. This can be adapted to cover any type or group of media where it is valuable to discover where the coverage occurred. Ratings can be awarded according to the perceived value of PR media, and this will vary from one business to another.

Let us assume, by way of example, that – to you – the value of the coverage is in descending order down the social grade classifications of the British national press. The most points are awarded to the most valuable, and fewer points to others. The following chart gives readings for three different stories printed on different dates, irrespective of the volume of coverage. (This is important because a few lines in the FT might be infinitely more valuable to your PR campaign's objectives than a whole column in The Sun).

Other results may be measured by calculation. Press reports and feature articles often produce enquiries by telephone or mail, and these can be counted. Again, they can be related to particular sources so that you can see which are the best media to use. You may be able to encourage this by offering leaflets in your stories, and perhaps your address will be printed.

Some magazines deliberately encourage response to editorials by offering a reader service, printing coupons or reply cards and giving news items and features code numbers. This is part of their effort to help readers, create reader interest, and calculate response, and this can be useful to you.

If you are distributing films or videos you can ask those giving shows to give you audience numbers. You can then record the number of showings and the number of viewers.

Other figures can be calculated such as the number of people attending private exhibitions, seminars or other PR events.

Media Coverage Rating Chart

PUBLICATION	RATING VALUE	STORY 1	STORY 2	STORY 3
The Times	10	X	X	X
Financial Times	10		X	
Daily Telegraph	9	X		
The Guardian	8		X	X
The Independent	8		X	
Daily Express	7	X		
Daily Mail	6			X
Daily Mirror	2	X		
The Sun	2	X		
Score		**28**	**36**	**24**

There can also be very practical numerical results as with new share issues where PR has been employed. What was the take-up of shares? Was there over-subscription which is itself a measure of success, provided there had not been over-kill due to excessive advertising as we have seen with some privatisation flotations?

When a private company goes public, the success of the new issue may depend very much on the knowledge the money market has about the company, and the extent of goodwill towards it.

That may well depend on how PR has been built up over a period, and not just on the special PR for the occasion.

Some such flotations have flopped through inadequate knowledge and, in particular, confidence in the company which has gone public. Two such examples of poor response were Avis and the advertising group Lopex, while the absolute opposite happened with Geest.

Another form of qualitative assessment is the tone of what they are saying, and how they are saying it. Was your objective to overcome the hostility, prejudice, apathy or ignorance of the media? In your case you might say that's a likely story if the media are always getting it wrong about you. But that may be because you've never taken the trouble to use PR to put the record straight.

The IPR has taken the media to task for malicious or deceptive reporting. Complaints have been made by offended organisations to the Broadcasting Complaints Commission, the Independent Broadcasting Authority and the Press Council. Even the Government has complained to the BBC. Legal action has been taken against the media, including one successful case against a consumer programme. We don't have to put up with media distortions.

Drastic action is not always necessary and more cautious, diplomatic PR methods are usually superior and quicker. If wrong information is published or broadcast, it is usually better to try to convert the enemy into a friend. It is often wiser to write to an editor, pointing out an error, offering correct information, and asking him – politely – to get it right next time. Face is not lost if apologies are not demanded.

So, has there been progress in turning these negative attitudes into positive ones? For instance, Glaxo was once described as a sleeping giant until it was able to change this because the company was shown to be enterprising in marketing a new product. The shift in attitude can be judged by analysing monitored coverage rather than just measuring the quantity. But you do have to earn the new tone.

In the previous chapter we referred to opinion polls, image studies and communication audits to appreciate the situation before planning a PR campaign. These can be continuous forms of research, and the same kind of study can be repeated at six monthly intervals, or annually, to record the shift in awareness, attitudes or opinions. A percentage change may be an objective. Is the result below this desired percentage, meaning that there was a weakness in the campaign, or was the percentage gained or exceeded?

By checking this percentage result, and showing it graphically, a post-mortem is possible. If the result is disappointing, was too little spent on the campaign, were the wrong tactics used or did something unpredictable or not taken into account affect the result? If the percentage exceeded expectations, was too much money or effort expended or did something unexpectedly favourable influence the result?

Other types of research used for marketing purposes may also help to show the effects of PR, and PR questions can be included in consumer panel or omnibus surveys aimed at finding out who buys what, where and when. Dealer audits, which record brand shares by checking purchases and sales at retail outlets, may also reveal the effects of PR as well as advertising.

From what you have read in this chapter you may decide that there is more to PR than you had previously thought. While your business cannot do without PR, and while PR is a kind of company intelligence system, PR needs its own intelligence system which is research. Otherwise you are working in the dark, floundering in a media pool, and probably wasting a lot of money.

The object of this book, and especially these last two chapters, is to help you to use PR as the eyes, ears and voice of your business.

In the Appendices you will find the names and addresses of a number of organisations which you may now, or in the future, wish to approach for advice and information.

Appendix 1

Contact addresses and numbers
(with web addresses where known, as at August 2000)

Advance, (monthly information about press features), 2 Prebendal Court, Oxford Road, Aylesbury, Bucks, HP19 3EY, tel: 01296 428585

British Association of Communicators in Business, 42 Borough High Street, London SE1 1XW, 020 7378 7139, web: www.bacb.org.uk

British Council, 10 Spring Gardens, London SW1A 2BN, tel: 020 7930 8466, web: www.britishcouncil.org.uk

British Trade International, 1 Victoria Street, London, SW1H 0ET, tel: 020 7215 5000 (previously British Overseas Trade Board), web: www.tradepartners.gov.uk or via the DTI at www.dti.gov.uk

Campaign, 174 Hammersmith Road, London, W6 7JP, tel: 020 82674743

Central Office of Information, Hercules Road, London, SE1 7DU, tel: 020 7928 2345, web: www.coi.gov.uk

EIBIS International Ltd., POBox 308, Ramsgate, Kent, CT12 5DG, tel: 01843 821358, web: www.eibis.com. Distributes translated articles to overseas press for clients.

Hollis Press and Public Relations Annual, Harlequin House, 7 High Street, Teddington, TW11 8EL, tel: 020 8977 7711, web: www.hollis-pr.co.uk

Institute of Public Relations, The Old Trading House, 15 Northburgh Street, London, EC1V 0PR, tel: 020 7253 5151, web: www.ipr.org.uk

Institute of Public Relations Journal, IPR, The Old Trading House, 15 Northburgh Street, London, EC1V 0PR, tel: 020 7253 5151

International Association of Business Communicators, Brussels, tel: 0032 2743 1541, web: www.iabc.com

International Committee of Public Relations Consultancy Associations (ICO), Willow House, Willow Place, Victoria, London, SW1P 1JH tel: 020 7233 6026, web: www.icopr.com

London Chamber of Commerce and Industry, Examinations Board, Marlowe House, Station Road, Sidcup, Kent, DA15 7BJ, tel: 020 8302 0261, web: www.lccieb.org.uk Examinations in marketing, public relations, advertising, selling and sales management.

PIMS (London) Ltd., Pims House, Mildmay Avenue, London, N1 4RS, tel: 020 7354 7000. Monthly publication of media lists and information. web: www.pims.co.uk

Press Association, 292, Vauxhall Bridge Road, London SW1V 1AE, tel: 020 7963 7000, web: www.pressassociation.press.net

Press Gazette, Quantum House, 19 Scarbrook Roaed, Croydon, Surrey, CR9 1QH, tel: 020 8565 4448

Profile, the IPR members' monthly magazine (also available on the IPR web site). IPR, The Old Trading House, 15 Northburgh Street, London, EC1V 0PR, tel: 020 7253 5151, web: www.ipr.org.uk

PR Week, 174 Hammersmith Road, London, W6 7JP, tel: 020 7413 4429, web: www.prweek.com

Public Relations Consultants Association, 10 Belgrave Square, London, SW1X 8PH, tel: 020 7245 6444, web: www.prca.org.uk

Public Relations Year Book, PRCA, 10 Belgrave Square, London, SW1X 8PH, tel: 020 7245 6444

Appendix 2

Glossary of Abbreviations

AA	Advertising Association
ABC	Accredited Business Communicator (see IABC)
ABC	Audit Bureau of Circulations
ABSA	Association for Business Sponsorship of the Arts
ACORN	A classification of residential neighbourhoods
AP	Assiciated Press
ASA	Advertising Standards Authority
BAIE	Britrish Association of Industrial Editors
BTI	British Trade International
BARB	Broadcasters' Audience Research Board
CAM	Communication, Advertising and Marketing Education Foundation
CEO	Chief executive officer
CERP	Confederation Européen des Relations Publiques
CIO	Chief information officer
COI	Central Office of Information
EIBIS	Engineering in Britain Information Service
FMCG	Fast moving consumer goods
IABC	International Asociation of Business Communicators
ILR	Independent local radio
IPR	Institute of Public Relations
ITC	Independent Television Commission
IPRA	International Public Relations Association
IT	Information technology
ITV	Independent Television
JICNARS	Joint Industry Committee for National Readership Surveys
LCCI	London Chamber of Commerce and Industry
NPA	Newspaper Publishers Association

PAO	Public affairs officer
PIMS	Press Information and Mailing Servic
PIO	Public information officer
PPA	Periodical Publishers Association
PR	Public relations
PRCA	Press Relations Consultants Association
PRSA	Public Relations Society of America
QC	Quality circles
UNS	Universal News Service

Appendix 3

The IPR Code of Professional Conduct

Conduct concerning the practice of public relations

A member shall:

1.1.   Have a positive duty to uphold the highest standards in the practice of public relations and to deal fairly and honestly with employers and clients (past and present), fellow members and professionals, thc public relations profession, other professions, suppliers, intermediaries, the media of communications, employees and the public.

1.2.   Be aware of, understand and agree to abide by this Code, any amendments to it, and any other codes which shall be incorported into it; remain up to date with the content and recommendations of any guidance or practice papers issued by the IPR; and have a duty to conform to good practice as expressed in such guidance or practice papers.

I.3.   Observe this Code and co-operate with fellow members to enforce decisions on any matter arising from its application. A member who knowingly causes or allows his or her staff to act in a manner inconsistent with this Code is party to such an action and shall be deemed to be in breach of this Code. Staff employed by a member who act in a manner inconsistent with this Code should be disciplined by the member.

A member shall not:

1.4.   Professionally engage in any practice, or be seen to conduct him or herself in any manner detrimental to the reputation of the Institute or the reputation and interests of the public relations profession.

Conduct concerning the public, the media and other professionals

A member shall:

2.1. Conduct his or her professional activities with proper regard to the public interest.

2.2. Have a positive duty at all timcs to respect thc truth and shall not disseminate false of misleading information knowingly or recklessly, and take ppoper care to check all information prior to its dissemination

2.3. Have a duty to ensure that the actual interest, or likely conflict of interest, of any organisation with whichj he or she may be professionally concerned is adequately declared.

2.4. When working in association with other professionals or institutions, identify and respect thc codes of those professionals or institutions.

2.5. Respect any statutory or regulatory codes laid down by any other authorities or institutions which are relevant to the actions of his or her employer or client, or taken on behalf of an employer or client.

2.6. Ensure that the names and pecuniary interests of individual members, all dircctors, executives and retained advisors of his or her employers or company who hold public office are disclosed and recorded in thc IPR Register of interests. This includes members of either of the Houses of Parliament of the United Kingdom or the European Parliament, a local authority or any statutory body.

2.7. Honour confidences received or given in the course of professional activity.

2.8. Neither propose nor undertake, nor causc any employer, employee or client to propose or undertake any action which would be an improper influence on government, legislation, holders of public office or members of any statutory body or organisation, or the means of communication.

2.9. Take all reasonable care to ensure that professional duties are conducted without giving cause for complaints of discrimination on grounds of age, disability, gender, race, religion or other unacceptable reference.

Conduct concerning employers and clients

A member shall:

3.1. Safeguard the confidences of both present and former employers or clients: shall not disclose or use these confidences to the disadvantage or prejudice of such employers or clients, or to the financial advantage of the member (unless the employer or client has released such information for public use or has given specific permission for the disclosure), except on the order of a court of law.

3.2 Inform an employer or client of any shareholding or financial interest held by that member or any stafff employed by that member in any company or person whose services he or she recommends.

3.3 Be free to accept fees, commissions or other valuable considerations from persons other than an employer or client, if such considerations are disclosed to the employer or client.

3.4 Be free to negotiate or re-negotiate with an employer or client terms that are a fair reflection on demands of the work involved and take into account factors other than hours worked and the experience involved. These special factors, which are applied also by other professional advisors, shall have regard to all the circumstances of the specific situation and in particular to:

a) the complexity of the issue, case, problem or assignment and the difficulties associated with its completion

b) the professional or specialised skills required and the degree of responsibility involved

c) the amount of documentation necessary to be perused or prepared, and its importance

d) the place and circumstances where the work was carried out, in whole or in part

e) the scope, scale and value of the task and its importance as an activity, issue or project to the employer or client.

A member shall not:

3.5. Misuse information regarding his or her employer's or client's business for financial or other gain.

3.6. Use inside information for gain. Nor may a member of staff managed or employed by a member directly trade in his or her employer's or client's securities wilhout prior written permission of the employer or client and of the member's chief executive or chief financial officer or compliance officer.

3.7.   Serve an employer or client under terms or conditions which might impair his or her independence, objectivity or integrity.

3.8.   Represent conflicting interests but may rerepresent conflicting interests with the express consent of the parties concerned.

3.9.   Guarantee the achievement of results which are beyond the member's direct capacity to achieve or prevent.

Conduct concerning colleagues

A member shall:

4.1.   Adhere to the highest standards of accuracy and truth, avoiding extravagant claims and unfair comparisons and giving credit for ideas and words borrowed from others.

4.2   Be free to represent his or her capabilities and service to any potential employer or client, either on his or her own initiative or at the behest of any client, provided in doing so he or she does not seek to break any existing contract or detract from the reputation or capabilities of any member already serving that employer or client.

4.3   Injure the professional reputation or practice of another member.

In the interpretation of this code, the Laws of the Land shall apply.

Index